Divine

Appointments

Ernest Dyess

Acts 22:15

Divine

Appointments

Ernest L. Dyess

PEBBLE HILL PUBLISHING
Camden, AL

Scriptural references are taken from the *King James Version* of the Bible.

Divine Appointments by Ernest L. Dyess
ISBN 0-9641704-1-8
Library of Congress Catalog Card #98-91691
Copyright © 1998 by Ernest L. Dyess

Pebble Hill Publishing
4425 Highway 41 South
Camden, Alabama 36726

CONTENTS

INTRODUCTION

This is a sequel to *GOD, IF YOU'RE REAL, LET THE COW BE IN THE PEN WHEN I GET HOME*. After the book was published in 1994, I began to receive requests to write a sequel. A pastor in Germany, H. D. Fraund, wrote and encouraged me to write again. "It will keep you young," was his encouraging incentive. However, it was not what others were saying but rather the things God was doing that motivated me to write again.

I feel that each of the chapters in this writing was inspired by Him. I mention in chapter 22 that God was giving me material, one chapter at a time.

The sequel has taken three years to finish. My writing has been spasmodic, written in between many other activities. In my case, I think that is the way it was supposed to be. I've often stressed that God ordains lay people—to share our faith "As We Go." Lay men and women aren't called into the vocational ministry, but we are called to be part of the Great Commission. We can fulfill that call by sharing what Jesus is doing in our lives with those He puts in front of us each day.

When I am asked to sign a book, I usually add Acts 22:15. That was Paul's commission, sent by God through Ananias. He was to go and tell the things he had seen and heard. Every saved person who knows Jesus has a story to tell. That was my primary purpose in writing the first book and this sequel—encouraging Christians to share their testimony. While reading my story, I hope you will be inspired to share yours. You might go a step further and write a spiritual journal to your grandchildren. The story of your walk with Jesus might be the inspiration they need to make Him their personal Savior.

I am also aware that many moral people still struggle with the question about the reality of God. Even Christians sometimes have some moments of doubt. John the Baptist had his moment when he was discouraged and in jail. When John sent his followers to ask Jesus if he was really the Christ, Jesus said, "The blind receive their sight, the sick are healed, and the dead are raised." Christians, like John the Baptist, always get an answer about the Lord's reality. If you are in a low spiritual ebb, hopefully, God will speak to you in these pages as I share about His reality in my life.

To the person who hasn't yet decided about the reality of God and asked Jesus Christ for salvation, you can still have hope. The Bible says to each person is given a measure of faith. If you are willing to use that faith and ask God about His reality, you will get an answer.

He answered me after I prayed about His reality and a lost milk cow when I was only a lad. I believe He will do the same for a person of any age seeking an answer about heaven.

ACKNOWLEDGMENTS

God used many people who read *GOD, IF YOU'RE REAL, LET THE COW BE IN THE PEN WHEN I GET HOME* to encourage me to write again. Many readers took time to write a note. As they shared what the book had meant to them, and in some cases suggesting a sequel, I began to feel that God wanted me to write again. So all of you who read and helped promote the book had an indirect part in this production.

Again, as he did with the original book, Jim Bonner played a major role with the sequel by keeping me in the computer business. After the first book was published, my computer broke down. When Jim learned I was thinking about writing again, he modernized the hardware and it has been functioning ever since. He wouldn't accept pay for his work. "That's my contribution to the book," was his comment.

To the many churches, associations, newspapers, radio stations and civic clubs who invited me to speak or be interviewed, my sincere thanks. Also, to Dr. Henry Lyon III for inviting me each year to Shocco Springs to share my witnessing experiences at the Pastors/Deacons/Spouses Retreat. I met many new friends at the retreats who encouraged me deeply. Bridge Publishing Company went the extra mile in their distribution efforts. Rachel and I shall always remember their invitation to attend the Christian Booksellers Convention in Nashville. All of you helped make the book known which resulted in the encouragement to write again.

My sincere thanks to my fellow Christians, and my Pastor, Eddie Davidson, at the Camden Baptist Church for your faithful prayer support preceding each of my engagements. Thanks to many of my other Christian friends, including some jail inmates, who gave your prayers of support which led to the sequel.

I have heard it said that our strength is in our family. That has certainly proved true in marketing the book and encouraging the sequel. First, without Rachel there would have never been a book or a sequel. I don't know about other writers, but my confidence moves from one end of the scale to the other. Rachel was always there to keep me on an even keel. The role she played in the writing and promotion is included throughout this narrative. My sister, Jeanette Ryan, made sure friends in Baldwin County knew about the book. Everybody needs a sister like Jeanette. Steve and Denise, along with their spouses, Diane and Neil, made Papa proud with all their help and encouragement.

A special note of thanks to my granddaughter Ashley, now enrolled at Judson College, for her editing help.

Denise took upon herself the final editing and laborious job of getting everything in its finished form. My thanks to her for the many hours of preparing the copy for final publication. May the Lord richly bless her efforts.

My special thanks to Sue Sumner for proofreading and encouragement.

God sent Bruce Bigelow of Tupelo, Mississippi to paint and design the cover.

However, it was not my supporters, including many others not named, or myself, who made this book possible. Again I quote Psalms 127:1, *"Except the Lord build the house, they labor in vain that build it: except the Lord keep the city, the watchman waketh but in vain."* It was God who brought the events which are recorded in these pages and it is to His glory that the book is dedicated.

Dedicated to the Glory of God.

1

God Saves People Who Drive Worn out Cars

For I tell you that many prophets and kings have desired to see those things which you see, and have not seen them; and to hear those things you hear, and have not heard them. (Luke 10:24)

I heard the old car rumbling across the fish pond dam roadway. Then it changed gears as it crept up the hill toward the house, leaving a blue trail of smoke along the way. As I emerged from my shop, the driver got out without stopping the missing engine.

"I'm looking for the fella who has the engine for sale," he said as I decided he was afraid the car wouldn't start again if he cut the switch. His clothes were deeply ingrained with grease and his face unshaven for several days. But there was a warm twinkle in his eyes that made my heart immediately go out to him.

"It's not me that has an engine. What is the person's name?" I asked.

"I don't remember for sure, but I think it's something like Clapps or Tapps," he stammered.

"That's Ricky Capps," I said. "He lives in the house where you turned off the highway. But if he is not home, don't get out because he has some bad dogs," I warned.

He thanked me and was turning to make his way back to the car when I stopped him with, "Before you go, let me give you something."

"Yeah, I sure would like a mess of those collard greens," he replied as he looked across the drive at my garden.

"I want to give you something better than greens. I want to give you a set of my magic cards," I said as his eyes became quizzical. "Let me show you how they work. Choose any number between one and twenty-five and I will let the cards tell me what you are thinking."

I showed him the cards and he told me the ones which had his number. I went through my little act of placing the cards in my shirt pocket saying, "Speak to me, cards, and tell me the man's number."

"You chose twelve," I said. Before I could say more, he turned his back, walked the few steps to his car, and cut off the engine.

"This man told me what I was thinking without me telling him. Get out, I want to see if it will work on you," he said to the woman on the front seat,

2

whom he later identified as his wife. As she got out so did another man who was riding on the back seat.

After introductory greetings, I did the numbers game with them, then proceeded to tell how it worked. "Now here's the good part," I said. I explained that we had just played a game but the message on the back of the cards was the real thing.

"The question we all face is on the back of card one. 'Do you know for certain you have eternal life?' Do you know if you died tonight you would go to heaven?" As I asked the question, I could see the carefree expression of the numbers game fade from their faces into the sincere reality of lost people, as each one slowly shook his head.

The driver was the first to verbalize what I had already seen in all three, "No, I don't know that."

"Would you like to know?"

"I want to go to heaven when I die," was his ready answer. Nods of agreement came from the others.

"Okay, let's read the message on the back of the cards which explains what the Bible says is the road to salvation."

Starting with John 3:16, and continuing down the Roman Road, I explained God's plan of redemption for all mankind through the blood of Jesus. I was about to give the invitation, as I concluded the message on the cards, when I was impressed to tell about what happened to me almost twenty years before.

"If you have any trouble believing there is going to be life after this life, let me share an experience I

3

had in 1974. It was the day we finished building this house. I thought my life was pretty secure. I had a good job, my children would soon be through school, then I would be able to get out of debt, save some money and live the good life. But God showed me that night that our security can never be in this life. I had just gone to bed when my back began to hurt and my arms ached down to my fingers. I had a great weakness as sweat covered my face. I knew I was having a heart attack.

"My son came home early that night because God knew I would need him to help me get into the car while my wife was calling the doctor. I passed out here in the yard and fell over on the seat next to him. I think I died for a while that night and didn't come back to life until we were on the highway. After we crossed the dam, I seemed to be in the car but not in my body. By the time we reached the house where the Capps now live, I was hearing heavenly music.

"God wasn't ready for me then, but I know from the experience that it's going to be that way when He is ready. After we take our last breath on this earth, in the next instance we will be with the Lord —if we have Jesus in our heart.

"Would you like to ask Jesus to be your Lord, forgive your sins, and come into your heart and save you today?"

The wife was the first to reply, "You know, I have been thinking about this for a long time. I want to be saved and get started going to church."

"Yeah, I want that too but I don't think I'm ready," responded the husband when I stated that we had to be sincere with God and could not play games with Him.

"God doesn't do things by accident," I said. "We just read on the cards that the Spirit that brings salvation appears to all men. Do you believe God might have had a hand in bringing you past the house you meant to find? Is it possible He brought you here so I could tell you how to be saved?"

"I see what you mean. Yes, I want Jesus too."

I turned to the other man, I think he was the wife's brother, "You have heard everything that has been said. Do you want to be saved too?"

Without hesitation he said, "Yes."

Beside that old, worn out car, I prayed with them. Three poor people asked Jesus to save them, and in so doing became rich. As rich as anyone in the whole world as they joined Christ's people in becoming joint heirs to God's kingdom.

I've shared this story many times, including the Alabama Baptist Evangelism Conference. I believe it typifies what God wants all Christians to do—share the good news with those He puts in front of us. They may not be on our social or economic level, but, in God's eyes, we are all equal because we are all His creation. My family didn't have a car when I was growing up. It's not hard for me to remember that except for His grace, I too could be driving a worn out car.

Shortly after this experience, I attended the 1993 Pastor\Deacon\Spouse Retreat at Shocco Springs, Alabama. Dr. Harold Bryson, now with the Sunday School Board and formerly a teacher at New Orleans Baptist Seminary, was the main speaker. In one of his messages he related a story about a man who was driving an old, worn out van. I believe his experience relates to mine.

He said it was spring, time for the bream to bed but his boat battery had died during the winter. "When I went to a discount store to buy a new battery, I noticed a crowd and several policemen gathered around an old white van. They were laughing and talking and seemed to be having a good time which made me wonder what had happened. As I paid the salesperson, I asked what the crowd was about.

"An old man lived in the van and sometimes he stayed in our parking lot. We noticed it hadn't moved in several days so we investigated and found him dead in the van," she said.

Dr. Bryson said he paid for his battery and carried it to his car. Led by his curiosity, he joined the crowd around the old van. "Does anyone know his name?" he asked. "Does he have a family?"

No one knew much about the man, other than he lived in the van, staying in various parking lots in the area. "I'm glad I didn't know him. He was just a homeless old man," volunteered one bystander.

As the crowd continued to gather, the coroner, driving a new van, arrived and three men got out. They took a rubber pouch, put on gloves, entered the van, brought out his lifeless body, and not too gently placed him in the van.

"I couldn't get the old man out of my mind," Dr. Bryson said as he returned home and prepared his boat for the fishing season. "I wished I could have met him before he died. I found myself visualizing a visit to his parked van, knocking on the door, being invited in for a cup of coffee. The van was probably dirty and the coffee old; but I would have liked to hear his story. It could have been something like this, 'I was once a pharmacist, had a wife and children. But we divorced and I turned to alcohol. Now I'm just surviving in this old van. Nobody cares about me anymore. You're the first person who has ever come to visit. Nobody cares about me—but enough about me. What about you? What do you do?'

"I'm a teacher. I teach preachers."

"You teach preachers? What do you teach preachers?"

"I teach them lots of things. I teach them to care about people."

"Do you think they would care about somebody like me, somebody who lives in an old van?"

Dr. Bryson went on to say, as he continued his "might have been" conversation with the old man, that he was on his way to a retreat at Shocco Springs where there would be about 450 preachers, deacons and wives present. He concluded his message by saying, "The old man asked if there would be anybody there who cared about a man living in a van. He took a blank sheet of paper from an old notebook, 'If there is anybody there who cares, will you send me their name?'

Dr. Bryson's concluding words were, "Could I send him your name?"

2

Where the Road Forks

Therefore if any man be in Christ, he is a new creature: old things are passed away; behold, all things are become new. (II Corinthians 5:17)

I was working in the garden when I heard Rachel begin grinding the lawn mower starter. Finally there was a loud backfire but the engine didn't start. More grinding, another backfire. I knew the battery would soon run down so I made my way to the shed.

"Why don't you hold up trying to start it and I'll see if I can fix it tomorrow," I said.

"I wanted to finish cutting the grass behind the large flower bed before dark but it can wait," she replied while making her way back to the house.

I don't pride myself in my mechanical ability but I thought it would be a snap to get the mower going again. It had sounded the same way last spring. I couldn't get it started then and was about ready to take it to a repair shop when I mentioned the problem to my neighbor Steve Huff.

"It sounds like it has water in the carburetor. Drain it and it may run," he advised. After I followed his directions, it cranked immediately, and has continued starting throughout the summer. As I began my repair work the next day, I thought the same procedure would work again but all I could get was the occasional backfire. I soon gave up and decided I would have to haul it to the nearest shop twenty-five miles away. But this time God had a different plan.

Rachel's Sunday School class was having a picnic that evening and I casually mentioned my problem to Nettles Ivey and Irby Ratcliff while we were eating.

"We have a good small engine repair man in Camden now," said Nettles as Irby seconded his recommendation. I decided to take the mower to him the next morning.

Frank was the only person in the shop when I arrived in a light rain. We quickly got the mower unloaded and he began making a work order ticket.

"What's the name?" was the first question.

"Ernest Dyess, but I have a set of cards here which has my name and address. Let me give you a set. They have a little number game on the front. I call them my Magic Cards because they will tell me any number you select between one and twenty-five. Think of a number and I will tell you what it is."

He looked at the cards and we played the game.

"Your number is eleven, the same as the number of faithful disciples Jesus had when He walked the earth."

I showed Frank how the game worked, then quickly said, "But the real message of the cards is on the back. 'Do you know for sure that you have eternal life?'" I asked as I showed him the question on the back of card one.

Frank didn't answer right away as I added, "If you aren't sure of your eternal destiny, you can read the back of the cards and the Bible verses will reveal the road to eternal life. If you already know the answer, you can share the message with someone who doesn't. The world is full of people who don't know the way to eternal life. My name and address are on the last card," I said as I handed the cards to him. He copied the final information for the work order and began to examine the mower.

I told Frank about the lawn mower's symptoms and we began a pleasant conversation as he worked. It was easy to share the story of cards. The Holy Spirit led me to share my own salvation experience—the heart attack, the heavenly music, and my commitment to share Jesus following a Lay Led Revival several years ago.

Suddenly Frank stopped working and looked up. "I know what you are talking about. I met Jesus when I had a loaded sawed-off shotgun with the hammer back pointed at my head."

"Tell me about your experience, Frank."

"At the time I had a drinking problem. When things got out of hand, my wife and I would

11

sometimes have arguments. One evening I came home drinking and things got unpleasant. I left home driving my pickup through some back roads in Clark County, depressed and at the bottom of life. After driving a while, I reached behind the seat and pulled out the old single barrel shot gun that was always there. I didn't think life was worth living any more so I decided to end it right there in my pickup.

"I was about to pull the trigger when Jesus spoke to me. 'Frank, don't do that. Let me show you what will happen to you if you do. Let me show you hell which is where you will go.' Jesus gave me a vision of hell. I actually felt the pain of torment. It was not a pleasant experience. When He brought me back to reality, He continued His conversation. 'Frank, if you will follow me, I'll give you eternal life. I'll give you a good life on earth. I'll take care of you. When you get a little further up the road, it will fork. If you go left, you won't hear from me again. If you choose me and go right, I'll be with you always. The choice is yours.'

"I knew which road I would take before I arrived. I turned right and headed home. When I walked into the house, my wife looked startled.

"'Frank, what happened to you! Your face is glowing,' she said.

"Jesus changed my life that night. He took away the desire to drink. He cleaned up my speech. He helped my relationships. I am not perfect. I don't guess I ever will be. But I know Jesus lives in my heart and I am saved," testified Frank.

"After I was saved, I drove to the forks in the road again. I didn't notice it before but as I looked down the left road, I could see a cemetery. Overlooking the right road was a church. The right road and church represented Jesus."

By this time Frank was very excited as he continued to tell his story of his new life in Christ. I could see that "New Creature" Jesus promises to make into everyone who comes to Him.

"Frank, a few months ago I was invited to be the speaker for Men's Day at the Heritage Baptist Church in Pensacola, Florida. Some of the men from that church are having a retreat here at the Roland Cooper State Park, and they asked me to be their leader tonight. You have been a blessing to me and I know you would be a blessing to them. Will you come and share your testimony?"

Frank hesitated for while, then said, "I know that is what I need to do. Let me think about it." I found out later that Frank's problem was not a commitment to go, but rather to work out things with his wife so she could take care of an uncle and Frank's father, both almost bedridden, while he was away.

By this time Frank had removed the fly wheel from the engine. The timing key was broken in half. "I knew that was the trouble when I heard the backfire through the carburetor," he said, reassembling the engine. With a confident thrust he pushed the starter and the engine was running as good as new.

As I paid my bill, I remarked, "Frank, it's good to know we have an excellent lawn mower mechanic in Camden, but it's more important to have a Christian brother to share with."

"The Lord sent you. This morning, I was feeling kind of low and I prayed that He would send someone to talk to me."

On the way home I thought about Frank's parting words, "The Lord sent you." I remembered another time a few years before when my tractor had broken down and I was unable to make a minor repair. It resulted in a long drive to a dealership for a new part. God had wanted me to talk to a salesman that day, just as He wanted to bring Frank and me together today. I felt like I was in the center of God's will as I unloaded the mower and went into the house to make final preparations for the retreat. God had already given me the first part of my message and now He had added another illustration of "Witnessing As We Go."

I arrived early at the riverside cabin for the retreat. Frank was already there. The Lord warmed our hearts with His presence during the fellowship that evening. It began with a wonderful meal, including fresh catfish caught by some of the men from the Alabama River. I'd asked Jimmy Brock and Fred Sheffield to bring their guitars and lead in singing of favorite gospel songs. Fred and Jimmy shared brief testimonies as they introduced their songs.

But Frank's message was the highlight of the retreat as he shared his testimony of the saving power of Jesus Christ, adding more details than he had shared with me. I could feel the anointing power of the Holy Spirit as he spoke.

Just as He had promised, God is giving Frank a good life.

3

Learning Faith Through Another Catfish Crop

Now faith is the substance of things hoped for, the evidence of things not seen. (Hebrews 11: 1)

It's been almost twenty-five years since we began raising catfish. Raising catfish has been one of God's classrooms to teach me to trust Him more. I'm a terribly slow learner because this year's crop (1994) has been among the most stressful yet in finding the complete trust of His leadership during difficult times. Since the beginning when God said, "Go into the catfish business," each year has been a new teaching and learning experience. This year has been no exception.

Rachel and I strongly considered giving up fish raising last year after losing over half the crop to "winter kill." In addition, our long distance from processing plants is a disadvantage for marketing in high production years created by large new operations. But we had raised an excellent crop of large fingerlings, just enough to stock the pond.

"We can get them ready for market before the critical time of the 'winter kill.' Market demand will still be good if we can beat the main fall harvest," was my thought as we dried the pond during the late winter. I was optimistic as we transferred about thirty thousand fat fingerlings, weighing a tenth of a pound each, to the big pond in early April.

By August the fish averaged over a pound. They were ready for marketing. But the market wasn't ready for us. I had miscalculated the growth of the industry which centered near the processing plants. They weren't ready to make longer hauls when fish were plentiful next door.

About this time a late season dry period set in and I noticed the lake level dropping. I was exasperated when I discovered a large stream of water still coming through the overflow pipe even though the water level was several inches below the overflow. I thought the drainage valve wasn't sealed properly and made several efforts to seal it with wood shaving which had worked in other years. But the drainage stream increased and the pond level continued to drop as the drought continued. If I couldn't stop the leakage, or sell the fish, I would soon have a dry pond and dead fish and our several thousand dollar feed investment would be eaten by the buzzards.

Paul writes in Romans 5:1 about Christians being

justified by faith and having peace with God through our Lord Jesus Christ. I know, if my faith is where it is supposed to be, I will not be concerned about the difficulties of life and will always have peace through trust. But the struggle goes on and the making of a new creature may take a lifetime. Perhaps the writer of the November 10, 1994 devotion of *Today in the Word* published by Moody Bible Institute, clarifies our struggles. "But in addition to peace with God, Christ gives us hope that isn't dimmed by adversity (verses 3-4). Instead, trials strengthen our hope as God uses them to purify us and makes us more like Christ.

Desperate, I contacted an out-of-state processing plant that had purchased fish in the area. I was surprised when they expressed an interest and asked for fish for a flavor test. "Wait a week and send another sample. They are slightly off-flavor," was their encouraging response. After about three weeks, when I was sure they were on flavor, they had lost interest.

All the while, the pond continued to lose water. Steve Huff, my neighbor, suggested a cap on the backside of the drainpipe. On his off day from his regular job he brought his portable welder and we attempted the project, only to discover that the drain pipe was about rusted away and was almost beyond welding. But Steve, an expert machinist, got the cap partially attached, which slowed the drainage rate. As long as it held, the pond wouldn't go dry.

As winter approached, the rains began and the pond refilled from run-off. Then I discovered that it wasn't the valve leaking but there was a rusted out hole in the front part of the drainpipe.

Thanksgiving came and with it the time for the "winter kill." Today is December 1. I've called the processing plants again. They say they can use the fish later but offer no harvesting date. Should I keep calling? How much should I keep trying to do? Should I just say, "God, you know the situation. You let them call me when you are ready to sell the fish. In the meantime, you can keep the fish from dying. You can control the lake. I put it all in your hands."

If I were advising someone else, I'd probably tell them to just trust God. But it is not so easy when it's you and you wonder if you are doing all the Lord wants you to do.

I don't know what will happen. I'll write the conclusion when it happens.

It's now been several months since the fish crop episode came to its conclusion. Like all the rest that had preceded it, it was a successful crop. We did suffer considerable loss from winter kill and were unable to sell the fish until early spring. But the price was good and our yield was almost 50,000 pounds, which made up for the loss.

The drainage system had deteriorated so it had to be replaced. Rather than dig out the pipe which would have required removing half the dam, we installed a siphon system of two eight-inch pipes and stopped up the old twelve-inch pipe with concrete. We had a record setting dry summer and the pond did not refill until fall. The pond grew up in weeds so we could not have restocked in 1995. It seems the Lord is saying for us to put the catfish business on hold for a while. However, our fingerling crop was fair so we decided to sell them to other growers. I don't know what the future holds, but I do know that God has blessed us through the fish business all these years. We have what I always wanted, a country home overlooking the lakes and grounds which provide the setting for the pecans and muscadines. The twenty-five years of fish business helped make it possible.

I am thankful for God's voice in the beginning, "Go into the catfish business."

AERATING CATFISH LAKE

PREPARING FOR CATFISH HARVEST

4

Yes, I Believe in Angels

Be not forgetful to entertain strangers: for thereby some have entertained angels unawares. (Hebrews 13:2)

I have found one of the best places to share Jesus is in hospital waiting rooms. I developed a cataract in my left eye and have made several trips to the Northwest Florida Hospital in Pensacola to see Dr. Clevenger, my ophthalmologist. He and several other doctors share a general waiting room, which is usually crowded.

"While we're waiting, let me show you my magic cards," usually gains the attention of those nearby. God has given me some memorable experiences with this approach. But the witnessing experience I remember the most happened one morning in a small waiting room after eye laser surgery. I'll never know this side of heaven all that God was doing in that forty-five minutes. I'll describe as best

I can.

The early morning procedure hadn't been exactly what I expected. My whole head ached from the numerous bombardments of the laser as it moved back and forth across my lower eyelid. A nurse said I would have a 45 minute wait, then the doctor would look at the eye again. As I took a seat in the small waiting room, already crowded with a dozen people, I thought about the old adage I'd heard—"Minor procedures are what other people have; it's major surgery when you're the patient."

"Has anyone here ever had laser surgery for eye drainage?" I asked, searching for an opener to share Jesus while we waited.

"I have," said a smiling elderly lady. However, her daughter interrupted and said that her surgery was different from what I had just experienced, and that pretty much ended the conversation.

Directly across the room was another lady, holding a *Reader's Digest* in front of her face. Maybe God would use the magazine for my opener. "Pardon me ma'am, but is that a December, 1994, *Reader's Digest* you're reading?"

She lowered the book, looked at the cover, and replied, "No, this is an old 1993 issue," and resumed her reading.

"I was just going to comment about a very special Christmas story, written by a school teacher, in the December issue," I said. I was confident that the Lord didn't want 45 minutes to go to waste, when people with problems needed to hear about Jesus. "Have any of you read the article?'

Again, my smiling lady friend spoke and said

she had read it.

"The story took place in a very affluent school," I said as I began to review the highlights. "A migrant worker's son enrolled in the teacher's class one day. He soon won the friendship of all the students, as well as the teacher. He had a genuine love for everyone and taught them things about the real world they had never experienced. When Christmas break came, he told the teacher his family would be moving the next day.

"'I brought you a present,' he said as he took a beautiful hand polished rock from his pocket. 'I polished it special for you.'

"There's a lot more to the story but the theme is about a boy who had nothing, yet everything to give."

My smiling friend and her daughter, an attractive middle age lady, were absorbing my every word. Off to my right, a well-dressed man in a business suit looked at the floor. I was unable to gauge the interest of the others.

"It's a great story, but I know another trail the young boy left. That's what we do in life. We leave trails. Some people call them footprints. I know another place the migrant boy went," I announced emphatically, as I tried to arouse the interest of the others. "He's been to Pine Hill, Alabama, a town a few miles from where I live.

"In 1977, Fred Pinckard coordinated a Lay Revival Team for a four day visit to the Pine Hill Baptist Church. He stayed in the home of Miss Emma Lee, a schoolteacher. On her mantel was a beautiful polished rock, which caught Fred's attention. 'Where did you get this?' he asked.

"Fred, who later published her answer in his book, *Evangelism Fire Through Lay Led Revivals*, wrote that Miss Emma Lee said a migrant family had set up a tent by a creek near town. Their young boy came to attend her class. She asked the other children to be nice to him, because he wouldn't be with them long. Her children always exchanged gifts at Christmas. When the day came, he brought a large paper bag, saying he had something for everybody. As he made his way to each child's desk and handed out a polished rock, she could see the child grasp the gift, as though it was the greatest present ever received.

"Miss Emma Lee said she thought of all the hours he spent wading up and down the creek to find the rocks, then the multiple hours to polish them, as he gave the rock on the mantel to her.

"No, I don't know where the boy is now, but it had to be the same boy who gave the rocks in both stories," I concluded.

"Maybe he was an angel," said the daughter of my smiling friend.

"Do you believe in angels?" I asked.

"I sure do," was her quick reply.

"Let me tell you an angel story I heard a few weeks ago. It had its beginning right here in this hospital," I said as I took a set of my special magic cards from my pocket.

"Usually I come to the hospital with enough of these cards to give everybody a set, but today I'm down to this last one. I call them my 'magic cards' because they can tell me a number you might be thinking, or in some cases, people's age. After playing the number's game with someone, I turn the cards over and read a question, 'Do you know for sure you have eternal life?' If a person is not sure, I invite them to read the Bible verses on the back of each card which explain the way of finding eternal life.

"On the day I heard the angel story, I came here early for an 11:00 o'clock appointment. I showed the cards to several interested patients in the main waiting room, then a pretty young lady came and took a seat right in front of me. She too was interested in the cards as I told her age. But it was a different story when I asked if she knew about eternal life. In no uncertain terms, she let me know that it was none of my business. I felt terrible. If there had been a hole, I would have gone in it. But God gave me a way out. Just as our confrontation reached its peak, the nurse came, and called my name.

"After seeing my doctor, I stopped at a McDonald's on the way home. Even though it was past the peak lunch hour, I didn't feel like sharing the cards with the waitress. As I began to eat my sandwich in the almost vacant dinning room, a young woman, I took to be the hostess, began to chat with me. Her friendly smile and warm words made me forget my recent unpleasant experience. Soon, my invitation to see the magic cards came out naturally.

"I thought she was about twenty years old so I asked if I could tell her age. She was 29. I congratulated her on her youthful appearance, then asked about her assurance of eternal life. She readily responded that she was not a Christian, but had been thinking about Christianity. We began to discuss the Bible verses on the cards and talked about God's plan of salvation.

"When I gave an invitation, she responded, 'Can I do it at home?'

"I told her I had been saved in the middle of the ocean; and God would save her in her home, if she was ready to give her heart to Jesus.

"'I'll do it before I go to bed,' was her promise as we rejoiced together before I left.

"Getting in my car to drive away, I realized I didn't feel bad anymore. Joy had replaced my unpleasant feeling of a short while ago. I had one more stop to make before the three-hour drive home. Raised near the gulf, I had cultivated a taste for fresh mullet, and usually bought some when visiting the coast.

"Just as the young man finished weighing my order at the fish market, a lady came in and wanted almost the same amount. We both wanted them filleted.

"'While we're waiting, let me show you my magic cards.' God's victory at McDonald's had restored my confidence.

"She played the game and did not hesitate informing me that she was a 'born again' Christian. In fact, she took over the conversation for the rest of our waiting period. I was the one being witnessed to, as she told of her walk with the Lord.

"'I have two daughters, one lives here and the other in Port St. Jose. A few weeks ago, my

Pensacola family and I went to visit my daughter in Port St. Jose. On the way back, the car stopped running. I told them we better pray and ask God to send someone to help, because my son-in-law doesn't know a thing about cars. He had barely steered the car off the highway when an old white pickup truck pulled in behind us. A man got out and said he was a master mechanic, and maybe he could help us if we were having trouble. He didn't look like a master mechanic to me. His clothes were greasy and dirty, he hadn't shaved in a week, and he didn't have any tools. All he had was a pair of vise-grip pliers and a screw driver. Nevertheless, he and my son-in-law got under the hood and he said the alternator had gone out. With nothing but the pliers, he soon had it off, and he and my son-in-law were on their way to find a new one, while we waited in the car.

"'My son-in-law said the parts clerk turned on his computer and said they had sold the last one they had that morning. It would be the next day before they could get another. 'What about that one on the shelf?' asked the mechanic as he pointed to an alternator behind the clerk.

"'How did that get there? We keep all our parts in the back. It looks like the one you need. Looks brand new. If you want to try it, I'll sell it to you,' was his comment.

"'When they returned, he soon had it on. 'When the alternator goes out the battery runs down, but a good battery may build back up. Try it,' he told my son-in-law.

"'It cranked right away. He left it running and

got out to pay the mechanic. He wasn't to be seen. The highway was straight and flat in both directions, but that pickup was no where in sight.

"She looked me straight in the eye, put both hands on her hips as ladies will sometimes do when they want to stress a point, and said, 'Now what do you think about that?'

"That was my first chance to talk since she took over the conversation, and I was speechless. Finally I said, 'Well, the Bible talks about angels, maybe he was an angel.'

"'That's what my twelve-year-old grandson said. He said 'Maw Maw, I'll tell you something else. He was the one who put the alternator on the shelf before they got there too.'"

The Digest lady was still shielded with her book, although she never turned any pages, and the man in the suit still stared at the floor. I turned to the daughter and asked, "Do you have an angel story to share with us?"

"I sure do," was her quick reply.

"I always did a lot of volunteer work at the hospital where my children were born, so I knew all the nurses and doctors. I already had two young children when I became pregnant again. When I went for delivery, I met a young woman who was there to have her first baby. I never saw anyone more excited. She told me all about their preparation for the child, the new nursery they'd built, everything.

"Delivery time came for me and I had a shocking experience. Without any advance warning, I had not one, but two babies. I was devastated. How was I going to manage and take care of two babies when I already had two children so young. After the family went home that night, I was still in shock when a nurse came into the room. She must be a new nurse, I thought, because I hadn't seen her before. She didn't say anything as she adjusted the curtains. At that moment I thought about the young girl who was in labor when I came in. I asked the nurse about her child.

"'Her baby was stillborn.' was her answer. Those were the only words she spoke as she left the room.

"In a flash, a light came on. I have two healthy babies and this woman has none. From that moment, I never worried again about raising them. They're grown now and every thing always worked out just as well as it would have with one child.

"I asked about the new nurse the next day. None had been hired. I described her to everyone I knew. Nobody had seen her.

"I know God sent that nurse to speak to me, to change my attitude. I believe she was one of His angels."

She got no argument from me, as I saw the sincerity written all over her face. The small cross she wore around her neck was not there for a decoration, but to glorify Jesus. "Would you like to have this last set of cards?" I asked.

"I teach a young boy's Sunday School Class; I believe they would love the numbers game," she answered. I showed her how the game was played and found out she lived in Gonzalas, a nearby town. She didn't tell her name.

"We've been doing all the talking. Does anyone

else have anything to share?" I asked, making another effort to bring others into the conversation. Nobody responded.

After a long silence, a wheelchair appeared in the doorway, and a nurse told a real old gentleman that she was going to leave him there for a while. He was rail thin, maybe ninety years old, but his warm smile could have camouflaged a hundred. I thought of another old gentleman, a self described, wore-out Baptist preacher, who had been used by God, in this same hospital to minister to a hometown man. This could be the same preacher, just older, I thought.

If I couldn't get the others to talk, I'd let them listen as I talk about the old man to my two friends, I decided.

"In the main waiting room this morning, I read a brochure summarizing brain tumor patients treated in this hospital. It reminded me of an experience I had a few years ago," I said as I directed my attention to my two friends. "I was coming home from work when I felt a strong impression to stop and visit a house I was passing. Some time before, I'd had the same feeling while passing another house, but I didn't stop then because I wanted to do something else that afternoon. I tried to make the visit later, but it was weeks before I could catch the family home. When I did see them, it was only a social visit. But I will always believe God had some special reason for me to visit that day. I didn't argue with God the second time around. I quickly stopped, drove into the man's yard, and found him at the end of his walk. It was almost as if he was waiting for me.

"I identified myself, told him I was from the Camden Baptist Church, and would like to visit a minute."

"Yes, your church prayed for my son when he was in a Pensacola hospital with a brain tumor," was his reply.

"I thought my son was going to die. As a matter-of-fact, I had just about given up one Sunday afternoon when I left his room to walk around the grounds. As I walked down the hall, I met an old man whom I hardly noticed as I passed. But he stopped me and said, 'I'm just an old wore-out Baptist preacher, but if you're having some kind of problem, maybe I can help.' I took him to my son's room and he put his hands on my son's head and began to pray. I never heard anyone pray like that before. Almost immediately, my son started getting better. Today, he's back at work and completely recovered.

"Why do you think that man came back that day?" he asked.

"God sent him back," I answered, "just as he impressed me to stop and visit with you today. Let me ask you a question. Do you know if you died today you would go to heaven?"

He dropped his head and said, "No, I don't know that."

I asked him if he would like to know. "I sure would," was his instant reply.

I took out my New Testament, read verses about God's plan of salvation, and gave him an invitation. There on his lawn, he prayed to receive Christ. He said he had been in Church a lot, even sung in the choir, but had never asked Jesus to forgive his sins and be his Savior. When I was ready to go, his parting words, spoken more than once, were, "Thank you for stopping."

I looked at the old man in the wheelchair. His smile seemed sweeter than ever. Again, I thought it was very possible that he was the same old Baptist preacher who had prayed for my Camden neighbor's son. As I glanced at the others, the Digest lady still had her book in place, and the well-dressed man looked troubled as ever. Then the nurse came and called my name to see my doctor.

As I was leaving, I turned my attention back to my two special friends and added, "About a month later the man had a heart attack and died; but I know I'll see him in heaven someday."

My forty-five minutes were finished. I felt God had led in sharing every story. Even though I saw no visible results, other than a warm relationship with my two friends, I believe the Lord was speaking to everyone in the room. After all, our job is to share the good news with those He puts in front of us.

Maybe the smiling lady and her daughter were also angels who were helping to share the good news.

5

Dog Stories While Witnessing

*My God hath sent his angel and hath shut the lions'
mouths, that they have not hurt me: (Daniel 6:22a)*

Fellow lay workers have reported many unusual
happenings while sharing the Lord. George Haun,
a dynamic layman who lived in Louisville,
Kentucky, told of an experience that has been
repeated many times at Lay Revivals across the
country.

Time has erased from my memory the place of
the story but I think it was in Tennessee. George
and a local church member had the name of a
person to visit who lived in a large house set back
from the street which was enclosed by a fence. They
parked on the street, opened a nearby gate and
proceeded up the long walk leading to the house.

About halfway to the house, a large dog came out of the shrubbery and fell in beside them. When they got to the porch, the dog lay down while they rang the bell. The man of the house was at the door immediately.

He looked at the dog lying peacefully on the floor. Then turned to the two men and said, "I don't know what you fellows are selling, but whatever it is, I want some. You're the first people this dog has ever let inside that gate."

I don't recall the results of the visit, but God closed the mouths of lions when Daniel was cast in their den. There is no reason why he will not also calm a dog.

Two other laymen shared about visiting a house and meeting a big German Shepherd on the front porch. They spoke a few words to him and decided he was a gentle dog and proceeded to ring the bell. When the residents answered and invited them inside, the dog also walked in, made a few turns on the carpet, and lay down. When the visit was over, the lay people made their way out the door and were about to leave when the mother said, "Aren't you going to take your dog?"

Maybe God also gives us some good dog company along the way.

6

The Old Super "C"—More Than a Tractor

He that tilleth his land shall have plenty of bread:
(Proverbs 28: 19a)

I felt tears might come, in spite of my effort to hold them back, as I positioned the trailer to load the old Super "C" Farmall tractor. But my neighbor, Steve Huff and his son Larry, drove up to help with the loading and the melancholy moment passed.

The old tractor, now over 50 years old, was more than an obsolete piece of machinery; it had become almost family. Its newly painted red frame and smooth running rebuilt engine had already survived three ownerships. It was a symbol of early American craftsmanship when things were made to last.

Its "heyday" had shined when America's "heyday" was at its greatest. Built at a time when we were creeping out of the dark days of the Great Depression of the thirties, it and other small one-and two-row tractors had relieved the drudgery of mule farming. It helped create the great strength of the family farm when morality and the work ethic of America was our greatest asset. It had its best days before the 'Bigger is Better' philosophy engulfed the land.

As Steve and Larry helped me adjust the wheels to fit the trailer, I thought back to a few weeks before when I told my son, Steve, that I was going to let him keep the Super "C". He had bought 20 acres of land, and was building a house, so I knew he needed a tractor. "It's part of the family. I'm not outright giving it to you, so you can't sell it," I had said.

Steve knew about it being part of the family. He was just a lad when I purchased the tractor and its equipment for $350 in 1966, shortly after we bought the farm while living in Suttle. He was with me on Saturdays and holidays when we cleared the abandoned farmland which had grown up in young trees. We would dig around a tree, cut the roots, then pull it down with the tractor.

Steve was also there when the Lord collected a tithe I had withheld the Sunday before. Rachel and I had made a commitment to tithe our income, but for some reason I had told the Lord that I would catch up my tithe later. Saturday came and we were ready to pull our first tree. It didn't budge. I gave the tractor more gas. The tires dug into the ground as they tried to grip the earth and pull the tree. Then there was the sound of breaking metal and one wheel fell half off the axle after its holding cuff broke loose. The price of a new cuff was the same as my unpaid tithe. The old tractor helped me learn that God expected me to keep my commitments.

As we secured the tractor to the trailer, I thought of how it was as much a part of Steve as it was me. That first cotton field of his had to be his remembrance. He felt insecure in his ability to plow the young cotton. "Daddy, you do the plowing. I'll plow up half the cotton if I do it," he requested.

"You can do it. It's your FFA cotton project, so have at it."

He plowed up a few stalks, but before it was over, he was doing pretty well. I think that, and other projects, helped give him the confidence that he could do things like anyone else.

When Rachel and I left early in the morning for the three hour drive to Steve's, I thought of the time I had brought the tractor to Camden after we moved, and how close I'd come to wrecking on the highway. I'd borrowed Bain Henderson's trailer and was doing fine until I topped a hill. I let the trailer get into a weave which carried me from one side of the highway to the other. The Lord kept other vehicles from coming until I finally regained control.

Just as it had been used to clean up the farm at Suttle, it became the tool to clean up the grounds around the ponds in Camden. "It's not a bulldozer," was Rachel's comment when I'd get it stuck or wedged between trees. But it had done the job until I was able to get a modern, more powerful, diesel tractor.

After I retired in 1988, my brother-in-law, Louis Hoggle helped me rebuild the engine. Neil, my son-in-law, brought his paint sprayer one weekend and gave it a new coat of International Harvester Red, then we added the dress up trim with new set of decals, and retired it as a garden tractor. When Steve bought his land in '92, it was time for the old "C" to go back to real work again.

Like father, like son, Steve has gone a step further and equipped it with grader blades which make it serve as a miniature bulldozer. I went to visit a while back and Steve assigned me the job of leveling a burned out brush pile behind the house. I think he kept the job just for me.

When I returned the Super "C" to its new shed, I could see the pride of ownership in Steve's face. I knew then the old tractor will continue to be around for a while.

When Rachel and I were driving home from Sylacauga, I thought about how God had used the old tractor to weave our family into a stronger unit while we were doing so many things together. The land clearing, collecting the tithe, growing the cotton and other crops, bush hogging, rebuilding the tractor, and a host of other activities all produced their precious moments. That's what the strength of family life is about—doing things together, building precious moments. God has indeed made the old Super "C" more than a tractor.

SUPER "C" INTERNATIONAL TRACTOR rebuilt after retiring.

7

I Don't Think I'm Doing It Right

For whosoever shall call upon the name of the Lord shall be saved. (Romans 10:13)

One of my objectives in writing *GOD, IF YOU'RE REAL, LET THE COW BE IN THE PEN WHEN I GET HOME* was to help any lost readers find the way to salvation. After the book was published, I received a searching letter from a lady in the military service who was doing a tour of duty out of the country. Following are some excerpts from the letter:

Dear Mr. Dyess,
—My reason for writing is because of your book.
—It really inspired me and I'm ready to turn my life over to the Lord. My only problem is I don't

think I am doing it right. I've prayed the sinner's prayer and asked the Lord to come into my life but I don't feel any different afterwards. I have heard many people talk of receiving a calling, or a great sense of warmth, after they commit themselves to the Lord and I've felt none of these.

In your book, you helped many people find the way to Christ so I decided to write and see if you can help me. —I hope you can help me find Christ.

Sincerely,

Lana

How each of us would answer a letter like this will reflect the way we share our faith in the market place. It might be good to stop reading for a few minutes and think about how you might answer such a letter, before you read my reply.

August 8, 1995

Dear Lana,

I was pleased to get your letter and learn that you want to make sure Jesus is in your life. Your experience of praying the sinner's prayer and inviting Christ into your life, yet not feeling different, is not an unusual result. The Bible says every person is given a measure of faith. I personally believe that is all we need to be saved, if we pray the sinner's prayer the best we know how.

Romans 10:13 says, *"Whosoever calls on the name of the Lord shall be saved."* That's a positive statement, not a 'maybe' statement.

The key is making Jesus Lord. Lord means ruler over someone. It means we surrender our will to

Jesus' s will. We make Him Lord of our life. If people are willing to make Jesus Lord of their life, and pray a prayer of confession of their sins and repentance (Romans 10:9-10), they are saved because the Bible says so. Only you and God can verify the sincerity of your prayer; but if you did the best you knew how, I believe God saved you.

Try to understand that being saved is not a matter of "feelings." It is pure faith in believing that Christ died for our sins, and through his shed blood we are made clean. We are saved by grace, or the goodness of God, because He loved us enough to give us Christ. (Reread John 3:16 and substitute your name for "world" and "whosoever") That makes it personal, Jesus died for Lana, just as He did for everyone else. It is through what He has done, not what we can do for ourselves. We can't add anything to what He has done, only believe and accept. Romans 5:8 says that "while we were yet sinners," Christ died for us. All Christianity hinges on Christ's death and resurrection. Jesus said, *"I am the way, the truth, and the life. No man comes to the Father except by me."*

I once had a neighbor who struggled with finding Christ in his late years. He thought he had to do something to gain honor with the Lord. He told me of reoccurring dreams, such as God being on a hill and his efforts to climb the hill to be where God was. "I was almost there, then the sand on the hillside caved away and I slipped to the valley below. It's always like that," he said.

I told him the same thing I'm trying to tell you, it's accepting what Jesus has already done for us rather than what we can do ourselves. He wanted to go to heaven, so he prayed the sinner's prayer, then said he felt no different. Like you, he thought there would be a "feeling." Sometimes people have such an experience but it is not synonymous with becoming a Christian.

Several months later, my neighbor was in the hospital to have an infected foot removed. Late at night he read the butterfly story in a devotional book. (The story is about a person chasing a butterfly but never able to catch it, then being still and it came to him.) It was at that moment he recognized he could not reach Jesus, that he needed to trust Him to come to him. And He did. "For the rest of that night, Jesus was in the room with me. I knew I was a Christian. When dawn came, He left."

My neighbor didn't lose his foot, only his big toe. From that day on, for the two years or so that he lived, he became a witnessing Christian. His life counted for Christ. When did he get saved? Was it when he first prayed, or that night in the hospital? Although I can't answer the question, I believe God honored his first prayer, then brought him to a point of understanding that salvation is giving up on self effort and a total surrender and trust in Jesus.

In conclusion, let me thank you for your trust in writing, congratulate you for your gift of beautiful handwriting, and assure you of my prayers that you will find peace with the Lord.

> In Christ,
> Ernest Dyess

Lana gave a forwarding address for me to send my reply. I don't know if she received the letter because I haven't heard from her again. I recently saw an interesting message on a church sign. Maybe its message fits Lana's situation. It read: "If you're searching for Jesus you may have already found Him."

8

Our Heavenly Class Reunion

Then said he unto him, a certain man made a great supper, and bade many: And sent his servant at supper time to say to them that were bidden. Come; for all things are now ready. (Luke 14:16,17)

Fifty-year class reunions, like Golden Wedding Anniversaries, are milestones for everyone who is fortunate to reach them. However there is another milestone that is far more important—our heavenly reunion with family, classmates and friends. Those of us who claim to be Christians, and feel comfortable that we are on the way to that glorious and final reunion, need to invite those about us to the great supper.

Several years ago I was invited to a Suttle High School class reunion. I don't remember their graduation year but I was one of the teachers of this very talented class. After most of the formalities of the program were over, Nelson Barnett came to the speaker's stand and gave a powerful testimony about what the Lord was doing in his life. Nelson urged everyone to make sure they had Jesus in their life. Recently, Nelson and I were talking about that class reunion. I was saddened to learn that some of the members are now deceased. I reminded Nelson that he had been faithful and invited them to the big reunion.

"Yes, it was the Lord who impressed me to do that," said Nelson.

Like Nelson, I had the opportunity to share Jesus at my fiftieth school class reunion. When we are looking ahead, fifty years is a long time; but looking back, it's like yesterday. The time had seemed even shorter to our Robertsdale High School Class of 1945 when we got together, through the efforts of Dorothy Cooper Martin, for our Golden Anniversary celebration October 20 and 21st in 1995.

Eleanor Hoiles Bankester and her program committee came up with the idea of doing a mock radio program, which supposedly took place in 1945, the last year of horrible World War II.

W. D."Dub" Hobbs, who acted as master of ceremonies for the program, and Frank Mathews served as WRHS radio announcers. Eleanor said in her introduction, "We are about to whisk you back 50 years to the most terrible, and also the most wonderful twelve months of the 20th century. So stretch your imagination, hang on, and enjoy a ride back into 1945."

The local and national news, reported by "Dub" and Frank, brought back memories of the war effort when everything was rationed; and the horrors of losing friends and loved ones in the war. In many ways, we were robbed of experiences kids usually enjoy in their high school years because of the raging war. But the little mock radio program helped us remember the good parts.

When Claude Hinote and Clinton Bankester reported our sports news, I thought about how our football team had been a bust, tying two games, but failing to have a single win. However, our basketball team was good. Only a three point loss to Murphy kept us out of the state tournament.

If our radio show had been judged for award winners, Louise Glass and Ruby Wallace would have been among the finalists after giving their recipe to cook Possum and Sweet Potatoes. Their fun recipe made us think of the Great Depression when rabbits, possums and sweet potatoes were still popular foods with many people.

Perhaps the highlight of the program was the radio commercials presented by various class members. Ads, which could only appeal to our hearing, (this was before TV), usually were accompanied by a melody such as, "Twice as much for a nickel too, Pepsi Cola is the drink for you." The smoking ads had the same remembrance. Our little program lived what advertisers know—bombard a child with a slogan and they will remember it for a lifetime.

Eleanor thought we should all give special remembrance and thanks to Mrs. Inez Hiles, our strict English and home room teacher who insisted we memorize parts of great classics from Shakespeare, Longfellow, Poe, and others. To relive our literature classes, Herman Ball presented Joyce Kilmer's "Trees," Dub did a comic version of Cleopatra, and I attempted a mini version of Hamlet.

It was a fun time for everyone to go back fifty years and relive the memories of our youth. But those days are gone forever, and no matter how hard we may try, we cannot bring them back. However, there is another way they can be relived to their fullest, and that is in eternity.

Several weeks before the reunion, I had been asked to bring the Devotional and Memorial for our deceased classmates. What do you tell a class of approximately sixty-eight year old people, many of whom you may be seeing for the last earthly time? After much prayer and deliberation, God led me to do the following:

"Two young boys, we'll call John and James, grew up in the same rural community. They played sports together, graduated from the same high school and were considered by their neighbors to be very close friends. As they grew older, they both married and started their own families. Their friendship continued through many community activities.

"One day, as John passed James' house on the way home from town, he saw a small wisp of smoke coming out of the gable end of the roof of James' house. John's first thought was that it might be the beginning of a house fire. But he rationalized that it was probably only smoke from a cooking fire. He also thought of the chores he had to do at home so he didn't bother to stop.

"That evening after John had finished his meal and settled in his recliner, the phone rang and a neighbor said, 'James's house just burned to the ground and he lost everything he had.'

"If James ever found out that John saw that first smoke, do you think he would still call him his friend?

"I've been asked to bring your devotional. If you've never found a personal relationship with Jesus, do you think you will still be my friend in eternity, if I fail to tell you about God's wonderful plan of salvation that assures us of eternal life?

"If you're still not sure there is life after death, you can find the answer by praying this prayer, 'God, if you're real, show me.' He has promised if you seek Him, you will find Him. I asked Him about His reality when I was about eight years old. It's not too late when you're 68.

"If you already believe there is a heaven and a hell, recognize that the smoke represents sin in our life. We are all guilty of displeasing God which is sin but in heaven there will be no sin.

God, because He loves us, provided the way for our cleansing through His Son Jesus Christ. When He shed His blood on Calvary, He redeemed all who will come and kneel at the foot of the cross and make Jesus Lord of their life.

"The Bible says in Romans 10:13, 'Whosoever shall call on the name of the Lord shall be saved.' When we make Jesus Lord and repent of our sin, we shall be saved, not maybe.

"If any of you are not sure about your eternal destiny, I have something that might be helpful if you will see me after the program. If you are sure, the material could be helpful to share the good news with others. You may have a friend or neighbor whose house is on fire."

I don't know if my class will have another earthly reunion or not. I can only hope that we will all be present for the heavenly reunion.

9

Write a Spiritual Journal

So shall my word be that goeth forth out of my mouth: it shall not return to me void, but it shall accomplish that which I please, and it shall prosper in the thing whereto I send it. For you shall go out with joy, and be led forth with peace: the mountains and the hills shall break forth before you singing, and all the trees of the field shall clap their hands. (Isaiah 55:11,12)

God has led me to meet some interesting and loving people during book signing engagements. One of my most unusual experiences happened at the Baptist Book Store in Birmingham. I had had a full day, first enjoying an hour long morning interview with Lester Hollans at WDJC Christian Radio, then a book signing afternoon at Books-A-Million in Hoover, before visiting the

Baptist Book Store for the evening engagement.

Phil James, manager of the store, had done a superior job of preparing for my visit. In addition to a catchy display of the books, a full-length poster drew many customers to my table. I didn't notice the couple at first, then the man presented two books for me to sign.

"This makes the 107th book I have bought," he said as he gave me two names for the signing.

I have somewhat of a hearing problem so I wasn't sure I heard what I thought I heard. "I don't hear real well, so will you tell me again what you just said?" I asked.

"This is the 107th book I have bought and given to various friends," he said as he introduced himself. "I'm Milton 'Sarge' Lester, recently retired from the Midfield Police Department. I heard your first radio interview with Lester Hollans at WDJC a few months ago, bought a copy, and have been sharing it with friends ever since. If you do speaking engagements, I would like to get you to come to our Brotherhood at Fairfield Highlands Baptist Church."

"When someone buys as many books as you have, they can get me to speak almost anywhere," I said.

That was the beginning of a great friendship. Sarge had lost his first wife, then met Kathleen, a charming lady who was attending their church. They were to be married that summer.

Sarge said he had been saved only six years. However, as I got to know him, I could see that he was sharing his faith more than many people do in a lifetime. I didn't have to stay around him long to see that his enthusiasm was contagious as he sought ways to serve the Master.

Norton Burgess, a former mayor of Midfield, had led Sarge to the Lord. "He and some others kept encouraging me and one day I knew it was time to make a commitment to Jesus," said Sarge.

Brother T. A. "Buck" Duke, Pastor of Fairfield Highlands Baptist Church, had received a book from Sarge and he invited me to speak at the morning worship service following the Brotherhood breakfast. The Lord usually gives me the theme for my talks well in advance. I felt His leadership as I made my preparations for the Brotherhood, but there was no message for the worship hour. God hasn't called me to be a preacher so I try to prepare all my talks from personal experience about the things I have seen and heard. But nothing seemed right for the morning service. My prayers for direction drew blanks.

After the Brotherhood breakfast and program, Brother Buck, as he is affectionately called by his membership, let me use his office to meditate. I related my frustrations to him. "That's the Devil trying to bother you before the service," was one of his comments.

When he left, there was still no direction. "Maybe God doesn't want me to be here," was my thought as I remembered telling Sarge that I sometimes spoke at both Brotherhoods and the morning service. Could I have invited myself? I promised God that morning that I would try to never make a statement like that again. If He wanted me to do something, He would open the door.

At the height of my despair, my attention came to a picture frame with a miniature violin protruding from its edge. My mind ceased its searching as I read the inscription. I can't remember the exact words, but the prose was about an auction which included an old violin. Nobody was willing to pay a dollar or two until an old man came from the back of the room, picked up the old violin and played a masterful tune. The auctioneer resumed the auction. Now what am I offered? A hundred, now two, and on and on the bidding grew.

"What made the difference?" the question was asked. Then answered by saying, "It was the touch of the Master's hand."

In that moment I knew I still didn't have the answer for my talk but I did have the introduction. I would have to trust God to guide me the rest of the way. I don't remember all the witnessing experiences and testimony I shared that morning, but I felt God's leadership after I told of my frustrations and the violin story.

I was glad to see several people renew commitments to be available for the Lord's use in witnessing during the invitation. Highlands Baptist Church members have a history of making commitments to serve God. One such lady, Rosell Hood, told me of an experience she had with the Lord about a year before.

"God asked me to encourage grandparents to write a Spiritual Journal to their grandchildren," she said as we talked following the service. "When

God's request came, I told Him I wasn't qualified—
that I didn't have much education. But the Lord
persisted, so I talked to Brother Buck. He thought
it would be a good idea so I talked to two of my
sons who are Baptist preachers. They too thought
it was great. One of them has a computer and he
began to help me make tracts for handouts," she
said as she gave one to Rachel.

"God has opened one door after another. I have
spoken at churches, been on radio programs, and
talked to people like you. If it's all right, I want to
write you a letter and tell you more about myself,"
said Rosell.

A few days after we returned home, we received
a ten page, hand-written letter from Rosell. I hope
she kept a copy because it should be part of Mrs.
Hood's own Spiritual Journal.

"God used a cow to reveal Himself to you; He
used a song to make Himself known to me," was
one of her beginning comments. She talked about
our generation being the last of those who lived the
'Great Depression'.

"My daddy was a coal miner but he couldn't find
work in Alabama so he was out of the state looking
for a job when one of my brothers took deathly sick.
We had no money for health care so Mama had to
spend all her time nursing him. When we got to
almost nothing to eat, a black lady who lived
behind a field near us, brought some chitlins to the
house and cooked them in our kitchen. That was
the best meal I can ever remember eating. After she
cleaned the kitchen, we went out on the porch and
she took me up into her lap. As she rocked me in

an old chair she began to sing very softly and sweetly, 'God will take care of you.' The song was more than words as she repeated it over and over. I was a very small child at the time and didn't become a Christian until years later, but God comforted me with those words through many difficulties until I found Him in a personal way through Jesus Christ.

"My daddy was killed in an accident three years later but somehow Mama managed to raise us in those difficult years. I married when I was fifteen and began to raise a family of seven children. You can imagine my surprise when God spoke to me at age 72 and said He wanted me to write a Spiritual Journal for my grandchildren, and to encourage others to do so. I argued with God but the message didn't go away, so that's when I went to talk to Brother Buck. It's been almost a year now and God has opened many doors for me to share my story to grandparents."

Mrs. Hood ended the letter by challenging us to be part of the team to encourage the writing of Spiritual Journals to grandchildren. I have thought a great deal about her message, even considering that God sent me to Fairfield Highlands Baptist Church mainly for the purpose of meeting Rosell. I've already shared her story at several speaking engagements, including one radio station. A few weeks ago I shared her challenge with a group of senior citizens at the Thomasville Baptist Church. "We all want to leave our children and grandchildren special gifts. Usually we think in terms of land, money, stock, homes and keepsakes;

but Mrs. Hood is right: the greatest, and only lasting gift we can give, is the way of finding eternal life through Christ. The story of our road to victory in Jesus might be the very tool needed for a wayward grandchild to find his or her ticket," were my concluding remarks that day.

I wished to know more about my ancestors when I wrote *GOD, IF YOU'RE REAL, LET THE COW BE IN THE PEN WHEN I GET HOME*; but the one person who knew much of our family history, my Great Aunt Sally, had died. I've regretted that I never spent time talking to her when I was young. However, while the book was being published, I had the opportunity to visit Betty Langham, Aunt Sally's daughter, who now lives near her son, James, in Jemison, Alabama. I was questioning her about our ancestors when she replied, "All I know is what I have written." Her journal consisted of 42 typed pages which gave me a clearer picture of my "roots" than I have ever known. It is a gold mine for me and my family which I will always treasure; it is family history, it is a Spiritual Journal. I think it's the type of writing God wanted Mrs. Hood to promote. Let me share a few excerpts.

Betty's grandfather, Winfield Scott Dyess Jr., was my great grandfather who settled a section of land in the Rosinton community about 1888. "We loved to sit and listen to Grandpa tell of his younger days when he first moved to Baldwin County from Monroe County. It took days for the trip in a covered wagon, bringing all their belongings: cattle, hogs, and all," said Betty as she wrote in her Journal about her youth.

"Mama, Papa, and I would go places in our 'top' buggy. There was just room for two in the seat and I would have to sit on a quilt in the front of the buggy. Sometimes I'd get them to let me sit on the back and I would jump off and run behind the buggy for miles. We would go to Stapleton through the woods. That's the way the roads were. Sometimes we would go to Magnolia Springs and stay for the weekend with Aunt Mollie Wallace. The roads were all three-trailed.

"I was seven when I started to Antioch School which was real close to our home. It was a one room school with long wooden benches and something in front to lay our work on. It was all crude, but up-to-date then. It had a wood heater, a bucket for water for all the children to drink from, and an outdoor toilet.

"Around 1918, cars began appearing in our community. Papa bought a roadster with no top and we felt very rich. Later, he and Uncle Jim bought a Model "T" touring car. We then took a trip to Monroe County where Mama grew up. Mama, Papa, Ted, Ada, their children and I went in our new car and I can't remember who went with Uncle Jim in his. It took the best part of a day to get there. The roads were all three-trailed and full of sand beds, but the pleasure we had was worth the trip. Seeing Mama's old home and where her mother was buried was very special (I never saw her).

"It was a little country church called Shiloh near Frisco City, Alabama. The cemetery was then quite small and the town was called Jones Mill. Mama's old home was between Frisco City and Excel.

"One winter (1918) there was an epidemic of influenza. People were dying all around with it. Of course, Papa and I took it. The Lord kept Mama well to wait on us. We had a neighbor, Mr. Eli Garner, who was the worst person in the community to get drunk and was rough on his family, but, bless his heart, he was an angel to help keep the chores done and keep plenty of wood in. What folks did in those days was for love and not money.

"Uncle Jim and Mr. Nick Hayes made caskets at the sawmill everyday. Lumber was always kept for that purpose, and it was free. Sometimes the caskets would sit on our porch all night. In those days when a person died, they were placed on a cooling board until just before they were ready for burial, before placing them in the casket. There was no embalming. Lots of folks died with the 'flu'; but finally the crisis was over and things returned to normal.

"...I've tried to give a picture of our homes and the kind of life we lived in those days, but one would have had to been there to imagine the peace and tranquillity we felt. There was no pressure to face; no bills to worry about; and no payments to make each month. There was less high blood pressure and fewer heart attacks. Those were such memorable days, even years.

"When I finished the eighth grade at Rosinton, which was a high school until then, they started busing the children past the eighth grade to Robertsdale. I met Aubrey Langham that year and we got married when I was fifteen."

Betty's journal continues as she tells the details of their early struggles just to accumulate the bare necessities of housekeeping. The reader feels the love she gives while raising her four children: James, Billy, Jerome and Virginia. Her grandchildren can't help but know that their grandmother was a very special person — because she took time to tell her story.

For the most part, her writing is about the happy times. However, into each life some rain must fall. "...Before Billy and Jerome went into the service, Aubrey and I both accepted Christ. So when things got rough, we knew we had a Comforter."

Betty vividly describes the anguish of a mother as she tells about her feelings while all three of her boys did time in the service. Billy, the second son, had finished a tour in the service, married and settled in Mobile, then was killed in an automobile accident soon after his discharge.

"I'll never forget that day as long as I live. It was weeks before we could realize our son was gone. I then wondered if he was saved, since he had never openly confessed Christ. It really worried me.

"One night after my nightly prayer begging God to give me a sign if he was okay, I had one of the sweetest dreams. It seemed Aubrey, James, Jerome, and I were at the cemetery where Billy is buried. I was crying and the boys told me to hush and pointed over the church. I saw the most beautiful white dove with a halo around it. Then in my dream, I saw Billy. He had on his uniform, even his cap. I believe God was showing me Billy was saved while in the service. From that time on I never worried about him any more, for I truly believe God answered my prayer."

Betty describes a lot more grief in her life: the loss of her mother, husband, a close nephew, and precious Aunt Lula; but her personal testimony sums up the hope of all Christians.

"We have lots of time to think about our Savior and we know He understands. I pray each day our family will grow closer to Him. We love each of them and know they are morally perfect in our eyes, but we want them to live in the will of God and be under the blood of the Lamb, so they will always be safe. And when we leave this life, we hope to be with all our loved ones in heaven throughout eternity."

This chapter has been about three people: Milton "Sarge" Lester, Rosell Hood, and Betty Langham. Each of them found Jesus in their adult years. Since their salvation, each has been diligent in telling others about how Christ has made a difference in their life.

Brother Andrew Goodwin, a Home Missionary in Montana, received one of Sarge's books. After reading it, Brother Andrew invited our lay team to Montana to help grow a church in Hungry Horse (see chapter 28). This is another example of how God multiplies His kingdom through each of our witness. The word never returns void. Neither will it return void for any grandparent who will take the time to write a "Spiritual Journal."

I firmly believe God brought me in contact with Rosell and Betty as part of His plan to encourage others to write a Spiritual Journal. It might be the way for your grandchildren, and perhaps many others, to find eternal life.

10

Valentines and Precious Moments

Beloved, let us love one another: for love is of God;
and every one that loveth is born of God, and knoweth
God. He that loveth not knoweth not God; for God is
love. (I John 4:7-8)

Most of us can remember the first valentine we received from one of the opposite sex. Mine came when I was in the third grade at Rosinton School. The young lady who gave it might have done the same for all my classmates, but it made me feel like I had a very special place with her. There were never any romantic moments to follow between Naomi Walker and me, but I'll always remember that valentine.   Fifty years after our high school graduation I saw Naomi again at our reunion. As we reminisced, I told her how good she made me

71

feel with that valentine.

My own story reminds me of another I heard about a first grader, who was busy with his colors and scissors, when his mother asked him what he was doing. "I'm making valentines for my classmates," was his answer. The project faithfully continued right on through the week until Valentine's Day.

His mother, like many good mothers, became concerned that her little boy, who was not very outgoing, might not receive any valentines and would be very disappointed after all his work. She made a batch of his favorite cookies to help ease any pain he might have, and was waiting at the door when the bus arrived after school.

"Not a single one, not a single one," were his words spoken to himself as he opened the door.

"Mama, I didn't miss a single one. I had a valentine for everybody."

I like to use this story when I am asked to speak at church Valentine banquets, because I think it emphasizes the true meaning of Valentine's Day— giving without expecting anything in return.

I'm sure the young boy's valentines, like the one Naomi gave me, made a lifetime 'good memory' for each classmate.

True Valentine's Day doesn't come just on February 14th. Since it is synonymous with love, a real Valentine's Day can happen any day. Valentine Days are those charged moments which bond us together in precious memories of love which we carry for a lifetime. Just as I will always remember Naomi's valentine, there are many other precious memories in our valentine chest of special moments.

For instance, I like to remember one of my first fishing trips with my father. I was a child of the Great Depression which left us short on the monetary scale; but we were rich in the things that really counted.

Daddy worked hard to supplement our meager family farm income by sometimes helping other farmers gather their market farm vegetables. One night he came home and announced that he and I were going fishing the next day. We would ride with Dick Dawson to Styx River and fish while Dick carried his vegetables to Pensacola.

Daddy rigged me a little pole and helped bait my hook with worms; and God sent a big old bluegill to be my first and only catch of the day. But I don't think the fish would have merited my valentine chest by itself. It was what happened when lunch time came that made it a precious memory. We were sitting under the bridge when Daddy took out his pocket knife and reached in a paper bag for a can of pork and beans. I don't remember anything else we had to eat but I'll never forget the wonderful taste of the first store bought beans I'd ever eaten. That lunch finished off a perfect fishing trip for a man and his boy. No Valentine card could ever take the place of that day.

Sometimes precious moments develop later from difficulties that weren't very charming when they happened. For example, the adults in my family didn't exchange Christmas presents as I grew up. Financial efforts were directed toward getting Santa to visit the children. After Rachel and I married, I was slow to realize that young wives, just like girlfriends, expect special gifts at Christmas as well as Valentine's Day.

Early in our marriage, Wayne Dubose, my new brother-in-law, and I were getting in some holiday quail hunting on Christmas Eve. The hunting was good, but we decided by late afternoon that we had better stop. We needed to get the girls something so they would know we were thinking about them. It was too late to go to Selma but Mr. Easter who ran the Suttle Estate general store might have something suitable. We were both still getting things for housekeeping so a nice bowl ought to be appreciated. We agreed that we should add something personal. A pair of bobby socks ought to take care of that. Mr. Easter didn't have any Christmas wrapping paper. No need to worry. We carefully wrote their names on the brown paper bags to make sure they each got the right present.

That evening the family gathered at the Hoggles' for the Christmas Eve meal. After eating, Johnny, the younger brother, played Santa and began passing out the family gifts. Things might not have been so bad if Clarice, Louis' s wife, hadn't opened her present first. She made a big show about the pretty skirt and sweater which Louis had ordered through his mother who worked at a ladies clothing store in Selma. Then came the opening of the bowls and the bobby socks. Ruby Nell cried and Rachel got mad. Wayne and I discovered the Hoggle family celebrated Christmas on a different level.

The bowl and bobby socks story has become a

family heirloom. A Christmas doesn't pass without it being shared. Precious moments often are born out of such episodes—because we love each other.

All too often, we are guilty of taking our love ones for granted. Sometimes all it takes to realize our self-centeredness is to be separated for a while. This came home to me in 1978 when I made a mission trip to the Philippines. I was part of a large group of over fifty preachers and lay people led by Gene Williams. My assignment was the main southern island of Mindanao.

I was paired with Calvin Fox, a missionary from Arkansas. Calvin, like myself, was a Vocational Agriculture graduate. God had called him to take his agriculture knowledge to help the Philippine people grow food while he was telling them about the love of the Lord. Calvin loved the people and he loved the Lord. He also loved his family. He taught me things about love while I was with him for two weeks in the remote villages. "When I officially retire, I want to bring Margaret to one of these primitive villages, build our house with native material and really show these people how they can improve their living conditions," was one of his comments.

I did some shopping in Davao City before we went to the mission field. I found a beautiful piece of embroidered pima fabric for Rachel which she would later use to make her dress for Denise's wedding. I knew she would be pleased with the fabric, so I thought my shopping was finished for her. But after two weeks in the remote villages, I began to think about getting her something more.

A decorative set of sea shell wind chimes made by natives caught my eye. I felt sure Rachel would like those. Again, I felt my shopping for Rachel was finished. Our final stop on the almost month long trip was Hong Kong. We had three days to see the sights before arriving home on December 23rd. By this time I had spent most of my money. As we visited the shops, I found Hong Kong to be a shopper's paradise, especially during the holiday season. It would sure be nice if I could bring Rachel something really memorable. Then I discovered they honor Visa cards there just like in the States.

I was fascinated by opal rings, although I didn't know much about them. A local missionary, who did a program for us on Hong Kong's famous harbor floating restaurant, was an expert in gems. He helped me make my selection—a beautiful opal, surrounded by a series of diamonds. "It is the fire in opals and the quality of the diamonds that make them valuable," he said as we made the comparisons.

For me, the whole trip was one I'll cherish for a lifetime. I hope that God was glorified because I went. However, if it had lasted longer, the farm might have been in jeopardy of a mortgage. Separation does make us more appreciative of our loved ones.

Precious moments sometimes come when we get that warm hug from a loved one. There are times when we all need to be hugged or held close. I'll never forget the time my two and a half year old granddaughter, Rachel, needed to be held close. It happened the day her twin sisters, Andrea and

Erica were born. She had been excited about getting babies—until she saw them brought to her mother in the hospital. As Denise held a baby on each arm, I could see the shock on little Rachel's face. For the first time in her life, she realized there would be competition for her mother's attention. She looked at the babies and her mother for a long moment. As tears formed in her eyes, she turned to her next source of strength, "Daddy, hold me. Daddy hold me."

But having someone to hold on to you is not confined to youth. We'll never be too old to feel electricity flow in a special moment. After retiring, I considered buying a four-wheeler. Finally, even though I had never even driven one, I made the purchase. I brought it home and was learning to ride on the farm where I had plenty of open room. When I gained enough confidence, I asked Rachel to get on the seat behind me for a ride. With some coaching, she agreed—if I promised to go slow. However, I discovered the faster I went, the tighter she held to my waist. It was a warm feeling as she made her squeals and I made the turns. It was a precious moment, in a different kind of way.

Valentine's Day had its origin as a secular holiday. It's made meaningful to Christians because of who God is and what He did through giving us His son Jesus. God is love. Jesus died for our sins to make us clean for heaven. That was the ultimate love. Our part was very clearly spoken by Jesus in Mark 12:30-31: "*Thou shall love the Lord thy God with all thy heart, and with all thy soul, and with all thy mind, and with all thy strength: this is the first commandment. And the second is like, namely this. Thou shall love thy neighbor as thyself. There is none other commandment greater than these."*

From a secular view, the dictionary defines love: "(1) A strong feeling of personal attachment; (2) A tender and passionate affection for another— usually the opposite sex." A layman brought these definitions to life during a Lay Led Revival at a Baptist church in Newnan, Georgia several years ago.

The husband of a respected young couple had become addicted to drugs and his habit was about to destroy their lives. The church had taken the wife under their wing and given her a job in the Day Care Program. The husband had moved out of the house during their separation but often came back in an abusive condition. She got a court order for him to stay away, but he came back and tried to burn the house—with the family inside—because she wouldn't let him in. He was arrested and in jail when the lay team came. One of the first laymen to arrive was sent to visit the husband.

"He hadn't shaved in days and his clothes were a mess," said the layman. "I tried to tell him about the love of Jesus for every person; but I was having a hard time getting him to understand that Christ did indeed love him.

'What is this love you're talking about?' was his question after a long while.

"Let me explain it this way. Have you ever loved your wife? I mean really loved her!"

"Of course I have! I still love her! That's why it's so hard to live without her now," was his instant reply.

"That's the kind of love I have been trying to tell you about, only Jesus loves you even more. He loved you enough to die for you and redeem you from all your sins," explained the layman.

"I see what you mean," said the man.

The layman later reported to the team that the Holy Spirit had made the prospect ready to listen, and in a few minutes he asked Jesus to come into his life and save him.

"I wish I could tell my wife what has happened to me," he said as he began to experience the joy of salvation.

"Maybe I can arrange it. I know the sheriff," said the man from the church who had accompanied the layman. He was back in a few minutes with permission to take the man to the church for a visit with his wife.

"Can I shave and put on clean clothes before we go?" He asked

Rachel and I had arrived at the church when the wife, a very beautiful woman, came out of the Day Care into the hall to talk to her husband. We saw the scene but didn't know what was happening until later. There was a long silence as they looked at each other before he told her of his salvation. Again, silence as they seemed to be unaware of those watching.

"Will you take me back?"

In her eyes we could see that's what she wanted all the time. Already, she was seeing the new creature God was beginning to make in her husband as they melted together in a long hug.

Needless to say, revival broke out in the church as members saw the healing power of God's love in their fellowship. A precious moment had been witnessed by those of us who were there.

We have all had precious moments. Maybe small ones, like Rachel and me riding the four-wheeler, or large ones, like the reunion experience I have just described.

I once spoke at a Valentine Banquet at the Elkdale Baptist Church in Selma. After sharing some of the precious moments I have written, I challenged everyone to each share their most precious memory with their spouse before bedtime. It might lead to another precious moment.

11

Come and See

And Jesus said unto them, Come ye after me, and I will make you to become fishers of men. (Mark 1:17)

A lady named Opal visited Alabama in the late summer of 1995 and vented her fury across most of the width of the state. We were not directly in the path of the hurricane but it blew down several pecan trees and her cross winds left many of our muscadine trellis posts at a tilted angle.

I spent several days cleaning up the orchard and on a pretty spring morning started the slow job of straightening the posts when my thoughts were interrupted by the sound of a large tractor beyond my creek bottom. "Ralph Reeves, who rents the adjoining farm, must be getting ready to plant a new crop," was my thought. However, as the tractor got closer, I began to distinguish the sounds of a heavy bush hog at work clearing brush under the power line leading to our house. The tractor grew silent when it reached the fence separating our farms but the noise was soon replaced by the loud blare of three chain saws cutting the brush in the creek bottom. I was glad to see the REA crew maintaining the line because we sometimes lost power during summer thunderstorms when a limb or tree would be blown on the line.

I needed a hammer to re-nail an irrigation support wire so I headed for the shop in my pickup. I was about to go back to the vineyard, when I saw two men knocking on our door.

"How can we get our tractor here? We need to trim some of your pecan trees which are touching the wires," one of the men said without introduction.

"Our power comes in the back way but you'll have to go to the highway and come in from the front," I answered. We chatted a few minutes as the men told me they were contractors and not regular REA employees. This was their first time to work in this area.

I offered them a ride back to the vineyard. As they got out of the truck, I said, "I usually give everyone who visits a set of my magic cards. It's a little numbers game which I can use to tell how old you are."

When I asked their name, one of the men said Ernest. "I really like your name," I replied, then told him that was my name too. "Some people spell it with an 'a' but I spell it E-r-n-e-s-t." It was a fun time as I told his age, then turned to the second man and asked him to think of any number between one and twenty-five. He looked at each card longer than usual, but smiled and said, "That's right," when I told him his number was twenty-four.

"This has been a game, but the real thing is on the back of the cards," I said as I asked the question about eternal life. It didn't take long for both men to acknowledge that they didn't know about eternal life.

I read the Bible verses on the cards, gave some of my testimony, including my salvation at sea. Before giving an invitation to receive Christ, I usually try to emphasize that coming to Jesus Christ is more than saying words. We have to make Him Lord of our lives, repent of our sins and be willing to let Him make us into a new creature. I like to end my witness before the invitation by letting the prospect read Romans 10:13, with the emphasis on 'shall be saved,' not 'maybe.'

When I showed the verse to the second man and asked him to read it, he slowly shook his head and said, "I can't read." My heart went out to him because it had not been my intention to cause embarrassment; but I knew he was too close to receiving Christ to talk about his disability.

"You know numbers, but you have trouble reading, so let me read the verse to you. It says, 'For whosoever shall call upon the name of the Lord shall be saved.' That means anyone who will make Jesus Lord can go to heaven. Would you like for Him to come into your life right now and save you?"

Both men accepted and prayed the sinner's

prayer. After I encouraged them to find a Bible-believing church, make their decision public, and be baptized, we had a prayer and they rejoined their three-crew members across the swamp.

Satan had lost two souls, but even in defeat, he wants to destroy the joy we have in seeing someone come to Christ. He began to give me thoughts that their prayer had been insincere. As I had done before, I told Satan that the job of any Christian is to share our faith, tell God's plan of salvation, then leave the results in the Lord's hands.

I went to the house at noontime for lunch, then settled in my favorite chair to read the paper when Rachel interrupted, "There's a truck outside and a man wants to see you."

I recognized Ernest as I stepped out of the house. Without hesitation, he told me why he came. "I told this man what happened to me, and he wants to talk to you about the Lord too," he said as a fellow worker got out the boom-truck they had brought to trim the pecan limbs. I knew at that moment that Ernest's conversion was real. When a person has a genuine experience with Jesus, he usually can't wait to tell someone else. Ernest didn't wait longer than his lunch hour to invite someone to go to heaven with him.

Again, I took a set of cards, read the plan of salvation, and told the man if he believed Jesus died for his sins, he could be saved too. There in my yard, the three of us joined hands as Jesus added another soul to His kingdom. When we finished praying, I remembered a package of Christian literature I had received from John Kaiser of Bible

Truth Publishers. I had met John at the Christian Booksellers Convention in Nashville in January. "I have some material I want to give you and all your other crew members. I'll bring it to the orchard before you finish pruning the trees."

Some of the material was directed toward new Christians. I suggested they encourage the man who couldn't read to go to night school so he could learn to read his Bible. In the meantime he could ask his wife to read to him.

That Monday night as I shared Ernest's story with the men at the Camden Work Release Chapel I said, "Homeless people who live in the cities sometimes live in pairs. When they separate and forage for food, and one of them finds a place for a handout, he goes and tells his buddy where he found it. That's what Ernest did when he found Jesus. That's what all Christians are called to do."

We recently worked with Fred Pinckard's Lay Led Revival Team in Pine Hill, Alabama. While we were talking about prison ministry during an afternoon discussion, Thelma Baird, a team member from Kentucky said, "It's great that many prisoners get saved when we witness. But if Christians were sharing their faith in the everyday world, people would get to know Jesus and never get into prison."

Marjorie McCoy from Grove Hill, Alabama sums up what Christians should be doing in a letter I received from her on March 19, 1996:

Dear Mr. Dyess,

Thank you for your exciting book on - *Let the Cow Be in the Pen--*. It is a delightful book and I

85

enjoyed every word. I thank God for people who are not ashamed to share their faith. It is such an encouragement to others. My husband is a shut-in and I'm with him all the time, but I can share my faith with those who come to fix our appliances— washing machine, TV, carpenters, etc. I have been blessed as much as anyone I've shared with. Thank you for your experiences and for showing the rest of us it is not that hard to do. May God continue to bless you and your family.

In Christ,
Marjorie McCoy

Marjorie's note, and comments from others like her, are indeed an encouragement to me to write about the things I see and hear. However, when God lets me see the conversion of a man like Ernest, I experience the greatest joy known to man. I praise God for letting me see a convert begin to carry out the Great Commission so quickly.

Twice in the first chapter of John are the words, "Come and see!" spoken. Initially Jesus said them to Andrew and another disciple when they asked where he dwelt. Again, the words were used by Phillip, after he told Nathanael about meeting Jesus. Nathanael replied, "Can any good thing come out of Nazareth?" It was then that Phillip gave his invitation, "Come and see!"

Jesus Christ can only be experienced by those who are willing by faith to "Come and see." If Christians will do the inviting, Jesus will help the lost to see.

12

Steve's and Rachel's Turkey

Ask, and it shall be given you; seek, and you shall find; knock, and it shall be opened unto you: (Matthew 7:7)

I was already awake from the light rain beating on the tin roof of our camp house when the alarm clock began its dance in the predawn darkness. "I'm going back to sleep," Steve said, as we both agreed it would be useless to hunt in the rainy weather.

I had roosted a turkey the evening before and I thought today might be my day after almost four seasons of failing to even get a shot. Steve had already killed his fifth, a season's limit, and he was going to be my ears and point me in the direction of the turkey if he gobbled. Now the rain was washing away another chance to rebuild my hunting ego. In bygone years, it was I who usually got the limit while Steve was learning to hunt. Now with stiff joints at age 68, (69 in slightly over a week), impaired hearing and eyesight, the worm had turned and it was the son who was bringing the most elusive of all game birds home. Papa could only offer his congratulations.

Turkey hunting became my most fantastic sport after I came to Suttle to teach Vocational Agriculture in 1951. The local landowners had banded together and formed the "Cahaba - Oakmulgee Game Preserve" and restocked their lands with deer and wild turkeys. The program was successful and after a few years the club began limited hunting.

The wild turkey is an elusive and unpredictable bird which challenges the hunting knowledge and calling skill of any experienced hunter. Its pursuit addicts man to the extent that wives breathe a sigh of relief, hoping their household will return to normal, when the season is over. Once a person has experienced the thrill of hearing the exciting gobble of an "Old Tom" announcing the dawn of a new day, he is usually hooked to the sport. The first gobbling, sounded while the turkey is still on the roost tree, will make goose bumps rise on most hunters; but the real excitement comes when the turkey is on the ground and in full strut. The head becomes sky blue, the wattles blood red, and the magnificent plumage is indescribable.

The challenge between man and the strutting tom is the name of the game. The gobbler often stays just out of shotgun range, as he attempts to lure what he thinks is the hen to him, rather than come to her. Sometimes a smart turkey may stop gobbling, circle the hunter and approach from a different direction. The slightest movement on the part of the hunter when the turkey is in sight will end the game, and a wiser bird will live to challenge another hunter on a new day.

One of the most fascinating aspects of the wild turkey is their unpredictable character. Some days they won't gobble; or may ignore the efforts of the best callers; but when success does come, it is the most satisfying of all outdoor sports.

It's hard for a successful hunter, even one with occasional success, not to develop an ego. But nature has its way of returning, even those who get their limits, back to reality. As I have gotten older, I have used physical handicaps, especially my hearing, as an excuse for failure. However, I still like to think that I can yet play the game.

About seven o'clock the rain stopped, and although turkeys don't usually gobble that late, I announced to Steve that I was going back to the area I had been the afternoon before.

"I am going to work on my sermon for tomorrow; then I am going to fish awhile," he said as I left with all my camouflage gear.

I circled the fish pond, then made a set up past the back field in the fifteen-year-old pine plantation. I made a few calls, not really expecting any activity, but I thought a gobbler might be coming to the four-acre field as they will sometimes do after a rain. In about fifteen minutes I moved on another quarter of a mile and sat down by a tree overlooking a hardwood bottom. I gave a few clucks on my favorite wild turkey wing bone caller which Henry Nettles, a long time resident of Wilcox County, had made for me before his death. I followed the clucks with the soft "yelp" of a turkey hen. Then I waited as I had done so many times before. I was not far from the place where I heard a turkey fly up to roost the previous afternoon, but I knew that turkey could be miles away by now.

I thought I saw something move along the crest of the ridge. Could it be a turkey? If it was a turkey, I was in perfect position. My gloves and camouflage netting left no skin exposed. My 12-gage Browning, with its full choke barrel across my left knee was almost on target already. I thought all these thoughts as I strained my eyes looking through the netting. My left eye, which has lost much of its sight because of glaucoma and a cataract, began to water. Another slight movement, and there it was, the distinguishable head of a turkey looking for his hen. Although I was positive I was looking at a turkey, I wasn't a hundred percent sure it was a tom. Hens sometimes come to the call of other hens. At this stage, it's a waiting game and the one who moves first is the loser. Finally, it was the turkey as he took a few steps, stopping behind a tree. It was my chance to bring the gun to my shoulder and point it to the little opening which would give a clear view when he made his next move. It wasn't long coming as I could see his beard and all his gobbler characteristics. The gun roared and the turkey rolled toward the ridge as his wings beat the ground. It was a clean shot and my four-year drought had ended.

As I admired the fine bird and thought of the gourmet fried breast we would enjoy, another thought quickly came to mind. This was really Steve's and Rachel's turkey. I knew without a doubt that they had both prayed that I would get a turkey, as they had seen me go and go, time and time again, without a shot.

"I don't really need to get one. I've killed more than my share over the years," I had said. However, I know they sensed my frustration as the years passed and they saw my ego falter, especially when Steve told his turkey stories and shared delicious turkey breasts with us.

Steve didn't go fishing and was waiting at the camp house after hearing my shot. I could tell that he was as excited about me getting the turkey as I was.

"This turkey·is like Glenda's deer. I know the Lord put him in front of me because you and Rachel prayed. I'm glad this time it didn't take me two years to realize it," were my remarks to Steve as he admitted his prayers and showed me a new way to dress the turkey with his head tied to a line. "You can skin him much easier than you can pluck the feathers," he explained.

13

Resurrection of the Syrup Mill

Jesus saith unto her, Thy brother shall rise again. Martha saith unto him, I know that he shall rise again in the resurrection at the last day. Jesus said unto her, I am the resurrection, and the life: he that believeth in me, though he were dead, yet shall he live: And whosoever liveth and believeth in me shall never die. (John 11:23-26)

Tall and strongly constructed, it stood as a bulwark beneath the trees, dominating the space in its red tinted color that had perhaps lingered for over a hundred years. "Today's paint sure isn't made like it used to be," was my thought as I admired how the color on the old sugar cane mill had lasted.

I sometimes wandered by the mill on my Sunday afternoon walks in the early years after we purchased the Pebble Hill farm and noticed that year after year, it seemed to defy time. The nearby furnace which housed the pan for evaporating the water from the cane juice and making syrup had long since crumbled into a heap of rock and vines. But the mill, mounted on four huge stones, beckoned for someone to bring a mule and put it to use again.

Somewhat of a history buff, I couldn't help but visualize how the creek bottom must have hummed with activity in the fall, when the first frost signaled the end of summer and the sugar cane growing season. It was more than a time to make a basic family food that usually graced every breakfast table and furnished the sweetening for mama's cooking. It was a social time that brought families together as they helped each other strip, cut, get the cane to the mill, then grind it into juice for cooking over the furnace.

Having been raised on a farm in Baldwin County where my daddy and his brothers owned a mill, I could see someone standing over the furnace, like my Uncle Jim Seay, who was the community syrup maker. Every community had its syrup maker. He was the boss. He knew when and just how much wood should be added to the fire. He had his own set of blocks that fit into the pan passageways that would regulate the flow of the juice. His skimmer, a dipper-like contraption mounted on a long handle, was always busy skimming off the impurities as the steam rose from the boiling juice, which slowly turned to syrup as it traveled back and forth in the narrow passage ways across the pan.

Uncle Jim was continually testing the syrup's consistency. When satisfied it was just right, someone pulled the stopper and the golden brown delicacy poured into bright new cans, ready to float freshly churned butter, and be sopped with big, brown, hand-made biscuits.

During my youth, most of the syrup was stored in gallon and half gallon cans. In earlier years, it was commonly put into wooden barrels. Because of its diverse uses, most families needed a lot of syrup. Daddy always kept thirty gallons for our family of six and sold any surplus. In addition to breakfast syrup, Mama used it instead of sugar for much of her baking, because we didn't have the money to buy granulated sugar during the Depression.

As I paused to look at the ruins of the mill, I was sure that a lot of barefoot boys, and girls too, had probably waded the clear creek, and drunk fresh sugar cane juice from a community dipper, as it flowed from beneath the old mill. Most rural kids didn't have candy very often as they do now, but one of my fond memories is taking my Barlow pocket knife, peeling and chewing cane as soon as it began to sweeten in late summer. However, the chewing was never as good as drinking the pure juice from that old aluminum dipper. When syrup making time came I couldn't wait for school to be out so I could get to the mill. Sometimes the bus driver would let all the children unload and get their fill. I am sure that kids who visited this old mill had experienced the same gleeful times I did.

Although I was fascinated by the cane mill, I didn't spend much time looking at its construction details. I had been around several of the old mule powered mills, but to me, they were all pretty much the same. Most mills had two or three rollers attached to a long tilted pole extending over the top of a framework. A mule was hooked to the end of the pole and the rollers turned squeezing the juice from the cane as he walked in a circle. I did notice that this one was mounted on a frame made of six by six-inch heart pine timbers, was adjusted by a series of wedges, and was bolted together by iron rods. I had no plans to ever make syrup so that was the extent of my interest. I did notice that it had a nameplate—"George Peacock Foundry, Selma, Alabama."

The years passed and the majestic old mill still stood, seemingly as solid as ever, though I did notice that a sycamore tree was growing within the frame. More time passed and one day as I walked that way, I didn't see the mill. Was I in the right place? Then I saw the sycamore tree. It was larger and brush had grown around its base. As I looked closer, I saw the metal rollers and the rocks, but almost all the wood was gone. I examined what little wood was left and could see that it was not the weather which destroyed the mill but a colony of termites who had made their ground-to-earth contact by building their tunnel up the sycamore tree.

I was sad because I felt the old mill was more

than wood and metal, that it represented a passing era in America's great history. I mentally whipped myself for not taking the time to remove the sycamore tree and building a little roof to keep it out of the weather. But it was gone now, and like the old cooking furnace, I wrote the mill off as passing history.

In the fall of 1995 I was visiting Rikard's Mill Park, located near Beatrice, about fifteen miles from here. The mill houses a water-powered grist mill which has been in continuous operation since the Civil War years. The water mill has always fascinated me and I wrote a feature about its history when I edited MacMillan Bloedel's publication, *Perpetual Harvest*. Since I wrote my article, the heirs had given the mill to the Monroe County Heritage Museum for a park.

While I was visiting, Kathy McCoy, the enthusiastic director, said they had found evidence that a syrup mill also once existed on the site. "We need to find a mill so we can make syrup again," she said.

"There is an old mill on my place but I think it is too far gone to be salvaged," was my comment. But Kathy's enthusiasm was contagious as she told about already having the promise of a mule to power the mill. Before I left, I agreed to look again at the possibility of rebuilding it.

Steve Huff, my neighbor, was visiting one day and we went to look at what was left of the mill. "It can be rebuilt," he said with assurance. That convinced me, because Steve is a master mechanic and millwright. I had some available time in the winter months and hauled the metal parts and what little was left of the wood to my shop. I didn't have much to go on, just two pieces of wood and what I remembered of the original construction. The four large rocks the mill had been sitting on gave the overall dimensions. I recalled that the whole structure had been held together with mortise and tenon joints. With that meager information, I didn't know where to start.

I visited the museum in Selma and asked what they knew about the George Peacock Foundry. The attendant immediately led me to a full-length painting of George Peacock in a Confederate uniform. I learned he was an Englishman who had been hired by the South to be the Superintendent of the Naval and Ordnance Works Foundry at Selma. An interesting half day at the Selma Library revealed that Mr. Peacock knew more about metals than anyone in the country at that time. He had already been in this country several years when the war started. When he came to Selma, he searched the state until he found the right quality of coal for his furnaces that made the cannons, shells, ammunition and ships that contributed to the South's war effort.

When the war was over, Mr. Peacock started his own foundry, specializing in brass as well as iron. He invented a self oiling railroad wheel which became known throughout the world.

Neil and Denise came home for Christmas, and being a civil engineer, Neil became interested in the project. He spent several hours helping clean the metal parts and make some beginning cuts for the frame. He went home and visited the Birmingham library, hoping to find that Mr. Peacock had patented the mill. "I found a plow he had patented, but not the cane mill," he reported. About this time Neil's company transferred him to Knoxville, Tennessee so I lost his help.

By this time I realized that in addition to the cane mill being a part of history, its inventor was even more so. If he built several cane mills and sold them in the area, maybe I could locate one through a newspaper article. I got some phone calls through an article Hollis Curl printed in the Progressive Era, but no one reported a George Peacock mill.

Finally I decided I wasn't going to get any help, so I started the base, using a heart pine sill, hued with a foot ad, that Bob Creswell gave me. There was evidence that the roller supports were mounted on 3 inch by 7 inch timbers. After that beginning, slowly one piece after another began to come together, much like a crossword puzzle. Jim Bridges had responded with treated timbers when I reached a critical place. Sam Wilkerson, Eldrige Stewart, and "Gee" Gullett helped with some of the mortise joints. Steve Huff and his son Larry made the cap, the only lost metal part, and mounted the pulling pole. My son, Steve, came home for the Fourth of July holiday and helped haul the large stones the mill rested on to the yard, and make the final assembly.

Almost six months from our beginning, we were ready to see if the mill rollers would squeeze cane juice from the few stalks of sugar cane I had saved.

My four-wheeler became our mule and we soon

had the juice flowing just as Mr. Peacock had designed. Many hours of work, plus the moments of not knowing what to do next had ended. I believe it's pretty close, if not exact, to the original mill. When the last stroke of the paint brush was made, painted red as in the beginning, I felt good that a place of history had been restored.

While all this was going on, I was making every effort to locate a syrup cooking pan to complete the mill, including placing an ad in the REA monthly magazine. Then I called Danny Averitte at Yellow Bluff, one of the few syrup makers still active. "My father-in-law, Mr. Campbell, had a copper pan. Since he died, I had a stainless steel pan made which I use. I'll donate his old pan to the park," he said. Joe Holly prepared the site and built the furnace.

The following weekend I made my usual Sunday afternoon walk around the lake. As I paused for meditation time by my pine tree, God seemed to give me the thought that I should write something about the mill.

"What can I write about a cane mill that will be of interest to people?" was my thought response.

"Use the analogy of how termites got into the wood with the help of the sycamore tree, then destroyed the mill. That's the way a person's life can be when they let sin in. Once sin is given free reign, it eats from the inside until there is nothing but a shell left on the outside, and then it too crumbles. But tell them there is a way out, and that way is Jesus. He's the Redeemer and Resurrector. You and others have resurrected the old mill. Jesus resurrects people when they come to Him. Tell them it is never too late to ask for resurrection."

The following Monday I made my weekly visit to the jail. I sometimes go to the jail not knowing what I am going to talk about. God brought the cane mill to mind as I addressed about fifteen men in the big bullring.

"Yesterday the newspaper had a story about a young man who was a star basketball player at the University of Maryland. He was drafted by the Boston Celtics and was going to make millions of dollars. But termites, in the form of drugs, had gotten into his life and he died from using cocaine before he ever played professional basketball. His life is similar to the old cane mill I've been rebuilding. Termites ate most of the wood, but I was able to make it like new again. Most of you are in here because you have let termites get into your life. Are you going to let them destroy you? Do you need someone to rebuild your life? Jesus can do it if you will let Him."

The expression on the faces of the men let me know that the message was getting through. As we continued on that night, I knew God was using the rebuilding of the cane mill for His glory.

RESTORED SUGAR CANE MILL

GRINDING CANE at Rikard's Mill Park using
the restored mill. Syrup making days are
the first two Saturdays in November.

DANNY AVERITTE COOKS SYRUP on the family's old pan donated to the park.

14

Queen for the Days

--Consider the lilies of the field, how they grow; they toil not, neither do they spin: And yet I say unto you, that even Solomon in all his glory was not arrayed like one of these. (Matthew 6:28-29)

The best seat in the house is at the end of our breakfast table, a seat I reserved for myself after we finished construction in 1974. The view is always magnificent for one who loves the country as I do. I may still be half asleep when I meander my way to the breakfast room, but once I start gazing through the double windows at nature's panorama unfolding around the lake in the background, I'm soon fully awake and anxious to get outside for the excitement of a new day.

In more recent years, Rachel's gardening ingenuity has given the view a new dimension. Starting in May and continuing through June, and to some degree later, we now enjoy seeing new "Queens For A Day" as a striking mixture of day lilies grace the foreground.

Rachel's main bed of day lilies, containing over a hundred different varieties of red, yellow, pink, plus every other shade imaginable, is located in between the house and the lake and in direct view from my breakfast seat. They each have a name, some are Biblical such as "Amazing Grace," or "Moment of Truth," the whitest of all varieties. Another, developed by an Auburn admirer, is dubbed "War Eagle." Her favorite and mine is a huge yellow we call "Mr. Grant." As the years passed, new varieties have come home as a result of visits to nurseries and looking at the catalogs. To make room, Rachel has expanded her plantings to places along the yard borders. But my breakfast chair still has the best seat in the house for viewing those blooms that open each morning for their day of glory.

For many years there was a TV program titled, "Queen For A Day." The program got its name from the day lily whose blossom is one of the most gorgeous of all flowers, but it only lasts for one day. The program tried to make the guest lady a queen for that day.

Rachel's day lilies have become more beautiful each year as she added new varieties and made new designs in her beds. As we talked about the flowers while traveling to church one day, the thought came home to me that I've been fortunate to live with a queen, not a queen for a day, but a queen for a lifetime. I say that not only because of the things she does for me but also because of the things she is always doing for others. A recent Sunday School lesson had to do with serving others. It made me think of how she has lived out that calling in her community. Flowers have been one of her many facets to reach out and make someone else's life brighter. When we moved to Pebble Hill she planted a bed of roses by the carport. She grows them with tender-loving-care, and year after year they respond with beautiful flowers, many which find their way to a friend's house or a person recovering from a bout of illness.

A jar of her special turkey soup often accompanies her bouquet. Rachel's turkey soup is sometimes a by-product of our church's Thanksgiving and Christmas meals. She likes to bring home the turkey carcasses that are left after the carving is done, cook them some more in a big pot, remove the last morsels of meat, then use the stock as a base for her soup. When all the vegetables are added, many which she froze or canned during the summer months, she finishes it off with the right touch of seasoning and spices. For the past several years Rachel has taught a ladies' Sunday School class. If a member is out sick for a while, Rachel may show up with her flowers and soup.

As I do my jobs on the farm, I think of the many hours Rachel spends working with her flowers— keeping the weeds in check, watering, controlling insects, and rearranging plants for best viewing effect. Each year I make pictures when the day lilies are at their peak. They get prettier every year.

But the one who is responsible for their growth is the real Queen, a Queen for a lifetime.

RACHEL DYESS with a cluster of her day lilies.

15

The Marked Bible

--Obey my voice, and I will be your God, and ye shall be my people: and walk ye in all the ways that I have commanded you, that it may be well unto you. (Jeremiah 7:23)

"Hi, my name is Clayton Carpenter. Your husband gave me a Bible when he and another man visited my home while I was living in Dayton, Tennessee in 1979," said the caller when Rachel answered the phone on New Year's Eve in 1994. "If he's still alive, I'd like to talk to him."

"Yes, he's still alive and right here," she said laughing as she handed me the phone. I must have looked pretty bad in 1979, was my thought as I began my conversation with Clayton. He didn't have to jog my memory even if it was over fifteen years ago. I have replayed in my mind many times the visit with Clayton and his wife, because I had not really wanted to give him my personal *Christian Life New Testament Bible.* It had been a difficult gift to give.

It happened while we were on a Lay Led Revival in Dayton. The local church member and I caught Clayton at home while he was taking a day of vacation. He was a cordial fellow and insisted that we eat some of the food he and his wife were canning. I don't recall what they were canning, but after I shared my salvation experience, I found Clayton was very confused about what the Bible teaches is the way to heaven. We talked at length, but I just didn't seem to be getting through to him. Then the Holy Spirit seemed to say to me, "Give him your marked Bible; it may help him understand."

I had purchased the *Christian Life New Testament* shortly after the Lay Team came to Camden in 1975. It had ten outlines of marked and underlined Scriptures, with footnotes explaining the major topics. One of the topics was, "God's Plan of Salvation." I had spent hours studying and marking the Scriptures pertaining to the subjects with a highlighter. I usually took the testament out of my back pocket and referred to the salvation outline when witnessing. "How could the Lord ask me to give away something so personal?" was my thought.

But the Holy Spirit persisted; "Give him your Bible" was a clear command.

"Clayton, if I give you my Bible with the outline about salvation, will you read it?" I asked, hoping he wouldn't be interested.

"Yes, I'll read it," he answered as I began to explain the outlines.

Back home, I questioned myself about whether I had really heard God say, "Give him your Bible." Maybe it was just an emotion of the moment, I thought. Nevertheless, I soon purchased another Bible, just like the one I had given Clayton, and again began to highlight meaningful verses.

I hadn't had the new Bible long before God began to deal with me about spiritual pride. God reminded me how I liked to open the old Bible when sitting by other church members, then holding it in such a way so they could see my highlighted Scriptures. I got the message loud and clear that I had been exhibiting spiritual pride. Maybe that's why God wanted me to give the Bible to Clayton. I've told the story more than once and confessed my shortcomings. Confession is indeed good for the soul.

I was getting ready to watch a ball game when Clayton called fifteen years after our visit. He rehashed the details of our visit, so he could tell me why he was calling. "I now live in Town Creek, Alabama and own a cattle farm. Many times I would drive out to the pasture, park under the shade of a tree, and read that Bible you gave me. I've found the Lord now, and I want to thank you for giving me the Bible. I have thought about calling you for a long time but I just never did. This morning I said I was going to do it tonight."

"Clayton, the Lord wanted me to give you the Bible for two reasons. First, He wanted you to have it so you could understand the plan of salvation.

Secondly, he wanted to help me break some of my spiritual pride because I liked to show-off those marked verses," I said.

"But those marked verses are what helped me gain understanding. They helped me find Jesus."

"I'm glad you called to tell me, but God was dealing with me too," was my answer.

Clayton and I talked on for some time as he told me about his family. He was especially proud of his son who is a leader in his church. After we concluded our conversation, I paused to thank God for the peace we have when we are faithful to follow the leadership unctions of the Holy Spirit.

16

Lord, What Do You Have for Me Today?

For thou shalt be his witness unto all men of what thou has seen and heard. (Acts 22:15)

Full sunlight flooded my bedroom when I awoke. It was a day I didn't have to get up early to spray the pecans, or the muscadines, or go fish for a big bass. It was a retiree's fringe benefit, a day to linger a while longer in the bed and think about what I was going to do. A prayer thought came to mind, "God, I wonder what you have for me today. Do you have something special, or will it be just another day?"

Rachel was already up and about her activities when I poured my cup of coffee. She joined me for breakfast and our morning devotional.   Then I headed for the lakes to feed our new crop of catfish fingerlings and the 4,000 caged stockers we have as an experiment.

We had difficulty selling recent crops of catfish, usually about 50,000 pounds, so we decided to cutback on the grow-out pond stocking rate and consider raising fish in cages. We plan to explore the possibility of developing markets for smaller volumes, over an extended time, rather than trying to sell the whole lake yield at once.

I had fed the fingerlings and was on the pier feeding the cages when a vehicle drove into the yard.

"Are you Mr. Dyess? I have brought you some chemicals," said the driver as I made my way back up the hill.

He introduced himself as Arnold Woodham, the Branch Manager of Helena Chemical Company. We visited for a while and he was about to depart when I told him I usually gave visitors a set of my "Magic Cards." We played the game, then I showed him the question, "Do you know for sure you have eternal life?"

"Yes, I know I am saved," he quickly said.

Before I asked him what he based his salvation on, I told him why I was giving people the cards. "My commitment had its beginning on July 1, 1974. I had a heart attack that night and almost died. If my son had not come home early and helped me into the car, I probably would have. I passed out here in the yard, but had an unusual experience after we crossed the dam you just crossed. As Steve drove toward the highway, it seemed like I left my body, but not the car. When we got near the house you passed, I began to hear very beautiful background music. God let me hear a little of the sound of heaven that night. The reason I heard it was because I asked Jesus into my heart when I was a young man of eighteen."

Before I could say more, Arnold interrupted, "I know what you are talking about. I have had an out-of-the-body experience too," he said as he took a tract from his shirt pocket titled "The Baptist Faith and Message."

"You must be sharing Jesus too," I said joyfully.

"When you began your talk, I decided to wait and see what you had to say," he answered.

"I have found that people are interested in our personal experiences with Christ. We are not giving secondhand information. For example, there is the carport where Steve helped me into the car. Right here is where I passed out and fell on the car seat. But enough about me, tell me about your experience."

"When I was twenty-one, a tractor turned over on me. It took a while for them to get it off. When they got me to the hospital, I was almost gone. I left my body and was in the upper part of the room watching the doctors and nurses work on me. My whole life flashed before me. I thought of my wife and child and was very sad because I wouldn't be here to watch my little one grow up. Then I was before Jesus, and He seemed to give me a choice of going back or staying. It would have been good to stay, but because of my child, I asked to come back. He told me to go, and I went back into my body."

I looked at Arnold and saw the sincerity in his

eyes as he concluded his testimony.

"Since I retired, I have written a book. When someone wants a personal copy, I include a favorite verse of Scripture, Acts 22:15. In that verse, Paul was told by Ananias what God wanted him to do, after he first made a commitment on the road to Damascus in verse 10. Ananias told Paul, 'God wants you to go and tell the things you have seen and heard.' I believe that's the reason God gave you and me the near-death experiences. He wants us to share them with other people who may be struggling about the reality of God," I commented.

"I know He is real in my life and I want to share the good news when I can. I live in Clanton and my wife and I teach Sunday School classes. Lately, we have been struggling with a problem, and this morning during our devotional, we completely turned it over to Him. Whatever happens will be all right. It is in His hands," said Arnold.

As Arnold and I talked on, I could tell that here was a man who is letting Jesus be Lord of his life. We had prayer together, then Arnold gave me his recommendation for controlling a grass problem in the fingerling pond and he was on his way to see his next customer.

"You made my day," were my parting words as I thought about how God had indeed made this more than an ordinary day.

17

Randy Waited on God

Therefore shall a man leave his father and mother, and shall cleave unto his wife: and they shall be one flesh. (Genesis 2:24)

"My husband is Randy Taylor who once worked for MacMillan Bloedel and lived in Camden. He is reading your book, and asked me to get you to autograph it, if convenient, while I am in Camden," said the lady on the phone.

I remembered Randy as a most unusual, nice looking fellow, who had been in my Singles Sunday School Class. I couldn't help but notice the girls making overtures to him, but he didn't seem to be impressed. I mentioned this seemly lack of real interest in the ladies to Randy on a weekend hunt at our camp in Perry County.

"If God wants me to have a wife, He will send her and I will know it," was Randy's reply. "In the

119

meantime, I don't think I need to be out hunting one."

I had depended on God to unite me with my own spouse, so I commended him on his theology; although I must admit that I did do some hunting until Rachel came along.

Randy, a native of Louisiana, was a forester who specialized in computer science. He liked the outdoors and duck hunting was his favorite hobby. One Sunday he came to class full of excitement and shared that he had been to Georgia the previous week and found the Lab puppy he had been praying for. He even had the girls thinking about motherhood as he told of his first night caring for his new companion.

I visited Randy at his rented house several times, and could readily see that the dog was more than a pet as he grew into maturity. Then came a sad day when Randy's dog died. After work Randy let his dog out of the yard for exercise and he was struck by a car while crossing the road.

I knew that Randy's dog was almost like a child to him so I went to offer my condolences. I had just finished writing about my half-breed bird dog, Bill, so I took a copy of the draft. Needless to say, we talked about dogs and how God gives them to us for companions. But like all life, they die and life goes on.

"I know you loved this dog but I believe God will give you another one," I said.

With a broken heart he responded, "I don't think I'll ever get another dog."

Randy changed jobs a few weeks later, moved to

Mobile, and I lost touch. Now, over three years later, I was about to meet his new wife.

I was impressed with Esther immediately. She was very beautiful and had that wholesome look which is a natural attraction to men for life mates. "You have a fine Biblical name," was my comment as she introduced me to her sister, Lucy, and explained that they had spent the day in Camden visiting another sister, Mrs. Robert Green.

I didn't wait long to share with her what Randy had said on our hunting trip, "I hope you know that you are a very special person."

"Yes, I like to think that I am very special," was her quick reply.

I knew I had made a poor beginning so I started over, "God made every person special, but what I want to tell you is how you are special in your relationship with Randy. I am sure you agree that Randy is a nice-looking man, so it was natural for our Camden ladies to seek his attention. However, he never seemed overly interested. When I commented, he informed me that he was waiting on God to send him the right woman, if He had one for him. You have to be very special because you are sent from God," I said as I saw the mist of tears in Esther's eyes.

After we chatted a while about Randy's current job, their recent marriage, and her family background, she told me that the dog story about "Old Bill" had been meaningful to Randy. "He shared the story with me and said it helped him through a difficult time. He did get another dog and I have a cat. We didn't know how they would do together when we decided to marry; but they adopted each other right away, even sleep together," said Esther.

"The Bible says that a husband and wife shall become one flesh. Maybe that applies to your animals too," I said as we laughed about Esther's congenial stories about Sebastian, her old rugged cat, and Buster, Randy's dog.

I further knew that Randy and Esther's spiritual family foundation was on good ground when she explained that each came from different denominations, but had agreed on a third church as their place of worship.

Families that worship together, stay together. To that slogan we can add, "When God brings a couple together, their marriage is built on a solid rock."

18

A Monument to God

And God saw every thing that he had made, and, behold, it was very good. And the evening and the morning were the sixth day. (Genesis 1:31)

Rachel and I were on our way to Shocco Springs, our Alabama Baptist Conference Center, where I was scheduled to lead witnessing conferences at the annual Deacons, Pastors and Spouses Retreat. We had started early and had some extra time. As we were passing through Childersburg, I noticed a DeSoto Caverns Park sign.

"Let's stop and see if they would like to stock our book in their gift shop," I commented to Rachel.

Three years earlier, Rachel and I toured the caverns which are named after the Spanish explorer, Hernando DeSoto. According to tradition, DeSoto visited the area in 1540 while searching for gold in the new country.

Indian history, both inside the caverns and in the surrounding countryside, abounds. I. W. Wright, an early Indian trader, chiseled his name inside the main cave in 1723. His name is still visible today. However, his invasion of the Indian's ancestral cave cost him his scalp and his life.

Prior to the cave becoming a park, an archaeological excavation in 1965 unearthed a 2,000 year old Indian burial which is on display in the cave.

The caverns had a role to play in the Civil War when the Confederate States used the main cave, which has little variation in its moderate temperature of 58 degrees, to make gun powder.

The caverns, owned by private interest, were abandoned following the Civil War. During the Prohibition Era of the Roaring Twenties, the Cave became a moonshine and "speak-easy" known as "The Bloody Bucket." After prohibition days, the place was mostly unattended.

Mrs. Martha Wheeler, owner of the local Days Inn in Camden, recently told me she and her teen-age friends sometimes visited the caverns when she was growing up in nearby Talladega.

"It was scary, but fun, to visit and explore the caverns with a flashlight. In those days, there was no development at all, just woods and unimproved dirt roads leading to the place," she said.

In 1912, Mrs. Ida Mathis and a number of friends purchased the caverns and surrounding land with the idea of mining the abundant onyx, a colorful, semi-precious stone. However, Mexican Onyx became popular and the cave was left dormant.

In 1960, Mrs. Mathis bought the other mining partners' interest. Her son, Allen Mathis Sr., recognized the potential value of the caverns as a tourist attraction and leased the cave to Fred Leyton, who started the show cave in 1965. Allen Mathis III is the present owner and is committed to making it a first class tourist attraction geared toward wholesome family entertainment. Several other interesting features have been added to the park; but the main attraction will always be God's underground gift of His creation.

Rachel and I had marveled at the beautiful interior formations during our visit three years before. It was a visit I almost didn't complete. I even stopped our guide, and thought of turning back, as we descended into the depths along an almost vertical, spiraling staircase which had been installed as a temporary entrance. Exploring caves would never be my cup of tea as I could almost feel the rocks in the shaft closing about me.

"We're almost there," said the guide with assurance that everything was all right. "We're having a new entrance made which will make it easy to enter. This is only a temporary entrance."

I felt my claustrophobia gradually fade away as we talked and I regained my composure.

We soon reached the bottom, walked through a narrow, low tunnel which opened into a fantastic new world of the Great Onyx Cathedral. Larger than a football field and higher than a twelve-story building, massive formations of stalactites, draperies, and stalagmites graced the ceiling, walls and cave floor. Stalactites, some over 30 feet long, seemed to melt into waterfalls and eerie pictures of imagination. Names have been given to many sections which are indescribable in their beauty, especially when viewed through artificial lights and leaping fountains of waters.

As I gazed at one of God's unique creations, I was glad that I hadn't turned back. Our group was small but it didn't seem to matter to our guide as he explained the history of each section of the caverns.

Today, three years after our first visit, we parked and entered the grounds midst a lot of activity. I soon found out that the park's annual Arts and Crafts Event, which usually drew several thousand people, was scheduled for the next day. A man interrupted his conversation with a small cluster of people and greeted us with a warm hello. "I'm Joe Beckham, Director of Public Relations for the Park."

"You're just the man I need to see," I said. "We're on our way to a Baptist retreat at Shocco Springs and stopped to see if you will stock our book, *GOD, IF YOU'RE REAL, LET THE COW BE IN THE PEN WHEN I GET HOME*, in your gift shop."

Joe said I needed to talk to Al, the owner of the park, and made contact with him on his radio.

Al soon joined us. He was an easy man to talk with, as I explained that the book was about the reality of God in every day life, including several witnessing experiences.

"You have some fine people who have endorsed the book. Frank Barker, the pastor of Briarwood Presbyterian Church, is a friend of mine. My son attends Briarwood School," Al said as he began scanning the contents.

126

Workers were coming and going. Some stopped to speak briefly to Al for instructions, as they prepared for the vendors who would soon cover the grounds. After each interruption, Al's attention returned to the book while Joe and I chatted.

"Al has spent a lot of money for advertising and getting ready for tomorrow. We are praying that the Lord will send us good weather, and I hope you pray for us too," said Joe. The forecast was for a front to move in that night, bringing rain with it.

"I hope the rain doesn't last long. We plan to visit our son in Sylacauga, after the conference break at noon, and go bass fishing," I said. "But you have a whole lot more at stake than a fishing trip. People don't turn out for an activity like yours when the weather is bad," I added.

"We'll try the book in the gift shop. You can leave a dozen copies," said Al as he completed his scanning.

"Before we go, let me give you and Joe a set of my 'Magic Cards.' They have my phone number on them if you ever need to get in touch," I said.

We played the numbers game and I explained how the cards were used to share Jesus. I didn't have to ask about their Christianity. It had been showing since our introduction. Joe had already shared that he was a part-time preacher. Al cemented his position when he said, "We want to do something to glorify God here at the park. I'm especially concerned for those people who do not believe in Divine Creation. I want to build some kind of monument recognizing God as our Creator."

The four of us spent an enjoyable few minutes sharing the reality of God in our lives, then I realized it was time for Rachel and me to go. I told them I would be leading four conferences about how we can share Jesus "as we go" and asked that they pray that God would lead me.

"Why don't we have that prayer right now?" said Al. Without regard to the people around us, we bowed our heads while Al asked God to anoint me, give guidance and wisdom, and be in our midst during the conferences.

When Al finished, I prayed, thanking God for Christian brothers like Joe and Al. The Lord reminded me to include in my prayer Jesus's Commission to the disciples to go to the other side of the lake - Luke 8:22. There was no way for the boat to sink. They were headed for the 'other side.' I asked the Lord to take us safely through life to the other side. I also asked Him to give good weather for their day tomorrow.

God blessed me throughout the weekend and I felt His presence in every conference. But the rain came Friday night and continued on into Saturday afternoon. After we arrived home Sunday afternoon, I felt compelled to write Joe and Al the following letter:

Dear Joe and Al:

It was a blessing to meet you on our way to Shocco Springs. It is not often that one gets the chance to meet Christian Brothers in the business world who are putting the Lord first, and are not ashamed of Him in public. God heard your prayer for me, and blessed during the witnessing conferences I led. During one conference, I shared the highlights of our visit as we talked about how we can share Christ in the everyday world—"as we go." I also spoke of my prayer for you to have a break in the weather for the Arts and Crafts day. I especially thought about you on Saturday morning as the rain continued until after lunch. I thought I had faith to believe that God would bring you a good day; however, it rained until we arrived in Coosa County about 2:00 p.m., so I expect it was a poor day for people to visit the park.

When things don't turn out the way we plan, I am reminded of Walt Milner, a farmer I knew in Dallas County. We were at a meeting and Walt told of losing about 35 top hogs that were killed in a wallow near a fence, when it was struck by lighting.

When I commented about his tough financial loss, he replied, "The Lord will give it back to me in another way—if He wants me to have it." Even though this happened many years ago, I have never forgotten his words and have found them to be true in my own life.

Al, I believe with your faith, you'll realize the same thing.

Sunday, Rachel and I visited Millerville Baptist Church where our son is the pastor. During Sunday School, I shared our visit and your thoughts about making a monument praising God for His creation. It so happened that one of the members, Becky Robertson, is a school teacher and planned to bring her class to tour your park the next day. She said she was glad to hear of your stand for Christ, and your plans to erect the monument.

You didn't say what you had in mind, but Genesis 1:31 could be used on the inscription:

And God saw every thing that he made, and behold, it was very good--

> Yours in His service,
> Ernest

I don't know how God will lead Al about the monument; but I do believe He will take care of us in life, as well as the business world—in His own time and in His own way.

If this story has inspired you to visit DeSoto Caverns Park someday, you can get additional information by calling the park at 205-378-7252.

On June 7, 1997, Al made the formal dedication of the caverns and the park to the Lord. Just as we discussed, he went to the depth of the cave and excavated a piece of onyx and brought it to the park entrance. A plaque inserted into the stone and inscribed with the words of Genesis 1:31, is there to meet each visitor and verify Al's belief that God was the creator of the caverns and the whole world.

Before he introduced special guests and his pastor who gave the dedication prayer, Al commented, "In my own way, this place has always been dedicated to God. I have invited you to join with us today in this formal dedication of the caverns and park to God's glory."

Rachel and I left with the good feeling that God had indeed been glorified.

DeSOTO CAVERNS PARK OWNER AL MATHIS AND WIFE, DANIELLE,
beside monument recognizing God's creation of the caverns.

19

Muscadines by the Case

And I will rebuke the devourer for your sakes, and he
shall not destroy the fruits of your ground: neither shall
your vine cast her fruit before the time in the field, saith
the Lord of hosts. (Malachi 3:11)

The last day of September, 1996, was a beautiful
morning. We had started the seventh week of
harvesting an abundant crop of muscadines. We
had been working since the crack of dawn and were
making good progress. I was picking the last fruit
from some Summit vines when a worker called
from across the rows and said someone wanted to
see me. It was two ladies from Detroit, Michigan, a
mother and her daughter.

"We have been here for a funeral and are on our
way home, and would like to buy some of your
muscadines," said the mother.

I explained that we didn't make retail sales on

the farm, that all our sales were by the 22 pound case. She responded that she wanted a case. They chose the Summit variety after sampling Fry and Supreme. When I carried the case to the yard, I was surprised to see the mother's husband in the car.

We chatted briefly before I explained that I gave visitors a set of my 'Magic Cards.' I noticed the usual quizzical expression on their faces as I got the cards from my truck. I guessed the daughter's age to be in her twenties so I asked permission to let the cards tell me her age. I missed her badly when the cards showed her to be thirty-six. I suppose I'm thinking everyone else is younger as I get older.

"You have a youthful face," I said as I explained how the cards revealed her age. "The numbers are a fun game, but the important part of the cards is on the back," I said as I reversed card one and read the question: 'Do you know for sure you have eternal life?'

"This is a question we all must answer." I said and paused for their reply. The mother quickly responded and said she was saved and on her way to heaven. I got the feeling she had been a Christian a long time. I turned my attention to the daughter. I didn't have to wait long before she confessed that she didn't know our Lord.

"You have made the first step toward being saved. No one can be saved until they confess their separation from Christ. Would you like for me to show you how you can have eternal life?" She consented to hear the Bible verses and we began to read about God's love in John 3:16.

I went through the plan of salvation written on

the back of the cards. I told of my heart attack and hearing the heavenly music, and pointed to my driveway where it occurred twenty years previously.

"Jesus can save you right here, just as he saved me in the middle of the ocean," I invited as I concluded the invitation in the tenth chapter of Romans. By this time the Holy Spirit was doing His work as tears ran down the young woman's cheeks. Without hesitation, she said she wanted to be saved.

The father had not spoken during the witnessing time and I had not felt led to ask about his relationship with the Lord. I knew it was time now so I asked him if he knew Jesus. The Holy Spirit had worked in his heart, just as He had in the daughter's.

"I'm just like my daughter. I haven't been saved either," he answered.

"Would you like to ask Christ into your heart too?"

"Yes, I think it's time for me to do that," he replied.

"The Bible says that every knee shall bow and acknowledge that Jesus is Lord. That will happen on earth, or in the day of judgment; but it will be too late to be saved in the day of judgment. Where possible, I like to help people come to Christ on our knees. Let's hold hands and get on our knees, here on the lawn, as we pray," I said as I reviewed the seriousness of what they were about to do.

I was between the mother and daughter as I led the sinner's prayer. I've never felt the presence of the Holy Spirit more than while I was in that little family circle. Again and again the mother squeezed my hand as her husband and daughter came to Christ. I didn't ask, but I feel God saved the mother's loved ones because of her many prayers for them. God simply let me use the magic cards to show them how.

We said good-bye and I went back to the vineyard, then remembered they had forgotten to pay for the muscadines. It didn't matter, God had paid me many times over in seeing the joy in the faces of a new family in Christ. I had just started to pick fruit again when I heard an automobile coming down our dirt road.

"We forgot something," said the daughter as she held out the money.

VINEYARD during growing season.

20

Lord, Give Her a
Singing Voice

*Before I formed thee in the belly I knew thee: and
before thou camest forth out of the womb I sanctified
thee, and I ordained thee.* (Jeremiah 1:5)

When the sonogram announced that Pam and
Eldridge Stewart's second child was going to be a
girl, family members began to pray that she would
have a singing voice. The couple's first child, Matt,
had singing ability but his interest had waned as he
got older and became interested in other things. It
was natural that this musically gifted family
wanted to see their tradition continued, so
grandparents and family members prayed for this
new addition to have a musical gift.

It didn't take long for the family to realize that
God had heard their prayers. Almost by the time

141

she could talk, Valerie was singing. When she was just two years old she did her first solo at her church in Montgomery, Alabama. She sang not just one song, but a medley: Jesus Loves Me; Oh How I love Jesus; and Oh How He Loves You and Me. From that time on, requests came regularly for the diminutive young lady to sing for special events.

When she was three, Eldridge moved his family to Camden and they began attending the Camden Baptist Church. Valerie captured the admiration of the congregation with her first presentation, "His Love is Deeper." Time and time again, she fulfilled requests from the church body, singing solo and with groups.

From Valerie's viewpoint, singing didn't seem to be any big deal. Eldridge was in my Sunday School class so I got to know the family quite well. Sometimes Valerie and I had a grown-up conversation. When I asked how she could remember her songs so well, she replied, "All you have to do is practice until you know the song, then sing it."

One Sunday Eldridge invited Rachel and me to have lunch with his family. It was then I learned Pam was Valerie's teacher, leading her in the repetitions until she knew each song. Eldridge has a great voice and sings in the church choir, so we were not surprised when the father and daughter entertained us with several duets after lunch.

Some months later, Eldridge and I were talking about Valerie's gift, and it was then he confided about the family's prayers for God to give her a singing voice. "There is another part to the story too" he said. "Her songs have always been gospel. Not long ago someone gave Valerie a country music tape and she couldn't sing it. I guess the Lord wants her to glorify Him through gospel songs."

Valerie is six now, (1996), and none of us know what her future holds. I believe God has His hand on her—just as He does all of us—and will continue to bless and use her great gift for His glory. Maybe Hollis Curl, Editor of the Wilcox Progressive Era, might have had insight when he classified her as, perhaps an angel, in an editorial he wrote after she sang the National Anthem at a football game.

The editorial was written during the final stages of a dirty, mud slinging, political campaign which he said had left him depressed with all the parties involved. I'll let the editorial speak for Hollis:

Yes sir, I was getting pretty depressed. ...But then something happened to restore my faith; politically and otherwise.

It happened at a Wilcox Academy football game a couple of weeks ago.

I remember I was standing beside the fence not too far from the North end zone.

My son, Mark, was there; so was his friend Joe McEvoy. The game hadn't started yet and the three of us were talking about hunting; bird dogs and such.

We paused, heads bowed, for the invocation. With a couple of step-grandchildren playing, our own "amen" was particular sincere. The next sound was not unexpected; the electronic crackle of a tape about to begin the National Anthem.

"Oh, say can you see, by the dawn's early light..."

I suppose that over a lifetime of high school football I've heard close to 500 renditions of our anthem; and that many more of various other venues.

I heard Roseanne Arnold disgrace herself on national TV with her raucous rendition, and there have been others almost as bad.

I heard Whitney Houston sing it pretty close to right but what I was hearing on the sideline of the Wilcox Academy football field was something else entirely:

It was the most genuinely stirring presentation I ever heard.

"…What so proudly we hailed at the twilight's last gleaming."

The voice was thin but pure; with the clarity of a child; or an angel perhaps?

I couldn't help but turn my head to the right to see who it was.

I looked first toward the press box but she wasn't there.

Maybe it's a tape, I thought.

Then I spotted her. A tiny little girl standing in the shadow of towering football players girded for battle.

She wore what I took to be a pee wee cheerleader outfit as she clasped the microphone.

"Whose broad stripes and bright stars ..."

I could feel a lump building in my throat.

The little lady continued as an uncharacteristic hush fell over the field.

There always seem to be a few fans who ignore

invocations and anthems as they continue their conversations. But not that night.

Every ear was turned to the little girl in the blue and white skirt.

The lump in my throat grew larger as I prayed silently that she wouldn't stumble on the high notes.

I didn't have to worry. She could have shattered a crystal glass with the clarity of her little voice.

"...O'er the land of the free, and the home of the brave."

Wow! The rampart Mark and Joe and I were peering over was a waist-high chain length fence. But I had no doubt that if Francis Scott Key had been standing beside us he would have shouted bravo when she finished.

The little girl never stumbled. Her enunciation was clear and precise. Every note was exactly as Key had written it; no pop music stylizing or Motown gyrations.

I asked a couple of folks standing nearby who the little girl was. They didn't know but their reaction had been much like my own.

Actually, it seemed it took the officials a second or two longer to whistle the teams onto the field. Everyone there was caught in, lifted up by, the little girl's proud voice.

I know her anthem was a personal blessing to me at a time when I needed the assurance that this is indeed the land of the free and the home of the brave.

I had begun to wonder if we had not—as a nation—become so polarized that we'd never get back together.

I know the answer now. I got it on the sidelines of a high school football game.

We'll always be one nation, under God, as long as there are little girls like 6 year-old, WA first grader Valerie Stewart to sing us the way.

Thanks Valerie. Thanks Eldridge and Pam for sharing your little daughter's talent with all of us.

I'll always treasure the moment she gave me.

(Used by permission from Hollis Curl)

Did Valerie get her singing voice because her family prayed?

I can't answer the question. I do know the Scriptures say for us to make supplications and our requests known unto God. That we have not, because we ask not.

Rachel and I sometimes pray for our five granddaughter's spouses-to-be.

Chances are the girls have not even met them yet. But they are out there somewhere, growing into manhood, and will someday be part of our family heritage. We pray that they will be Christians and spiritual leaders who will honor God by having a part in the building of His kingdom.

As Hollis has written, Valerie is already having a part in God's service. It was verified again at the Camden Baptist Church on the Sunday morning before Christmas, when she sang, "Happy Birthday Jesus."

I believe it's all happening because her family prayed.

VALERIE STEWART, at eight, two years after singing the
National Anthem at the football game.

21

God's Call by Way of South Africa

And I, if I be lifted up from the earth, will draw all men unto me.   (John 12:32)

I was helping usher at church when she appeared in the vestibule.

I gave my best "Good morning" as I presented the church bulletin.

Then she stopped right in front of me.   A somewhat apprehensive smile appeared on her face, as though she was waiting for me to say more.

I looked at the tall, sandy blonde lady with sparkling blue eyes and went blank. Perhaps in her early thirties, was she someone I should know?

I'd been embarrassed before when I had failed to recognize hometown girls who had grown up in our church, then left for college and careers. Was she one of those? Or a first time visitor?

After what seemed to me a long time, she turned, walked into the sanctuary, and took a seat on the back row next to Walt and Betty Chapman. I immediately asked Bill Bledsoe, my fellow usher, if he knew her. He didn't. I could see her talking with Betty and Walt and was glad. If she was an out-of-town visitor, they were making her welcome.

In a few minutes the service started. At the proper time we passed the offering plates, then I took a seat with Rachel near the front. I was bothered that I had done a poor job of welcoming our stately visitor. So I resolved to speak with her again after the service. However, by the time I got to the rear of the church, she was gone.

I did see Walter and Betty and found out she was a first time visitor, all the way from South Africa —but they didn't get her name.

On the way home, I told Rachel what happened and she was quick to say that we needed to make a follow-up visit. We called Dale Gaston, who meets all the new people at the power company, and she knew her address.

Tuesday evening we knocked on her door. A blond, blue eyed man with rather long, wavy, hair met us. When I introduced ourselves, he said he was Hermann Brandt and his six-year-old son was Carl. I told him we were from the church and presented our calling card, a bag of Pebble Hill pecans. Carl took charge of the pecans and was off to get a cracking tool. Then Wilmien came into the room and I began to explain why I had done such a poor job of welcoming her at church. "When I told Rachel what happened Sunday, she said we should visit and extend the right kind of welcome to our church. That's why we are here," I said.

They seemed glad to have us visit. Wilmien said she was here on a work visa as an occupational therapist at the local nursing home.

When I asked Hermann about his occupation, he replied, "I'm a professional hunter. I organize groups to go to South Africa to hunt. I am also a wildlife artist."

"What kind of game do you hunt?" I asked.

"Any kind people want to hunt. We specialize in buffalo, but all big game can be hunted."

I like to hunt. Hermann had my attention. For the next several minutes, we talked about the life of a big game hunter. Hermann had an album of color pictures of all kinds of vicious wild animals killed by hunting parties he'd conducted. If I was a mite younger, I might have been one of his first guests to sign up from Camden.

We talked about life in their country and their work here in the States. Then it was time for us to talk more about our church and the Lord.

"Your wife attended church alone Sunday. Were you unable to come with her?" I asked as I looked directly at Hermann.

Before Hermann could answer, Wilmien spoke, "Hermann doesn't go to church."

For a moment the room was awkwardly quiet, then I said, "Do you have some good reason for not going?"

"I was raised in the church. As a matter of fact, my dad is a minister. As I grew up, people

151

expected me to do certain things. I couldn't accept the mold other people wanted to put me into. I have decided I am going to be my own person," declared Hermann.

I had taken a set of the magic cards from my shirt pocket, with the intention of asking Hermann about his relationship with the Lord after playing the numbers game. I decided he had already answered the question, so I said, "I have some cards that have a little numbers game. Do you mind if I let them tell me how old you are? After they agreed, I revealed that they were both 33 and put the cards back in my pocket. It was obvious that Hermann couldn't be pushed. We talked awhile longer, then invited the family to our Wednesday night meal and prayer service. I told Hermann we would like to have him visit my men's Sunday School class, then changed the subject back to hunting.

On our way home Rachel and I discussed the visit. We both felt a warmth toward the family. Rachel fell in love with Carl. "He's so cute with his long eyelashes," she said.

"I believe God sent them here for a special purpose. I think He wants us to minister to them," I said.

I was somewhat surprised when they showed up at church for the Wednesday night meal. We ate together and made a special effort to introduce our church members. "He's a 'big game hunter' from South Africa," caught the attention of most of our men. Eddie Davidson, our pastor, gave them a warm welcome and they stayed for prayer meeting following the meal.

I thought I could get to know Hermann better if I could help him sign up some hunters. The Wilcox Academy annual deer hunt and later the spring wild turkey hunt bring a lot of wealthy hunters here. If he got involved with those it might help. I tried to get some of our men to take him to meet the hunt leaders. But they were all busy. Again, I felt the Lord wanted me to be the one. I presented the idea to Hermann, and told him I would pick him up the next morning.

Hermann brought his photo albums and they made an impression on Johnny Webb and George Fendley who were in charge of the respective hunts. Both welcomed Hermann to help host the events. I carried him to meet Hollis Curl, our local newspaper editor. Hollis and his son Mark, both avid hunters, went through the albums. Hollis took Hermann's picture and wrote an article about his hunting tours and wildlife art work.

After the paper was printed, Les Johnson, President of the Camden National Bank, invited Hermann to exhibit his paintings in the bank.

"You're getting to be the best known man in town," said Les.

As I drove Hermann back home after our visits, I felt I should leave him with a clear understanding of God's plan of salvation. "Hermann, I'm not going to browbeat you, but I do want you to know that I believe God is real, and that there is going to be life after this life. God sent Jesus who taught us the way of finding eternal life, and then died to redeem us from our sins on the cross. By His shed blood, death, and resurrection, we can have the gift of eternal life if we believe and ask."

"I believe there is a God, and I believe Jesus lived. If He wants me, then He can come to me. In the meantime, I am going to live my life in my own way," Hermann replied with no animosity toward me.

I parked in front of Hermann's house and made my final comment. "Hermann, the Bible says that Christ will draw all men to Him. Someday He'll do that with you. When He does, you just be sensitive to His call."

On my way home, I prayed my first of many prayers for Hermann. "God, reveal yourself to Hermann in a very personal way. I believe you have something special for his life."

Hermann and his family were usually present for the Wednesday evening meal and prayer meeting. He later confessed that he only came because he didn't want to cook. "Our visa doesn't allow me to hold a job. I can be self-employed, but can't compete for jobs in the work force. So I became the housekeeper."

The young couples in church took the family into their circle of companionship, inviting them to community activities. Everyone liked the family. They came to our Sunday School class dinner at our house. Hermann took an interest in the old syrup mill I was restoring, and he and Carl came to help make syrup when we tried it out. Wilmien and Carl attended Sunday School and church but Hermann only came on Wednesday night. Then one Sunday morning Hermann walked into my

Sunday School class—with a new haircut.

Sometimes in our Sunday school discussions, I ask overhead questions—a question anyone may answer. Although he was new to the class, Hermann often spoke, giving good answers. The next three weeks were like the first. I was trying to guide the lesson to interest a non-Christian, yet Hermann was acting like he already knew the Lord.

Because Hermann had been so upbeat throughout the lesson, I deliberately delayed him until everyone had left. "Hermann, has something happened to you since we last talked?"

We were late getting to church service that morning; but God made my day as Hermann told how God had made a personal visit to him.

"I was attending a business meeting in Dothan. The speaker had hardly started his presentation, when God spoke to me. 'Hermann, I love you. I am not the way you think I am. Just as you love your son, Carl, I love you the same way, only more. Just as you want the best for him, I want the best for you. I want you to be happy, fulfilled, joyful. But I also want you to be righteous. Hermann, is this what you want?'

"Yes Lord, that is what I want," said Hermann as he continued to share how God had spoke to him in Dothan.

"I remember the drive home clearly as I felt the presence of the Lord with me in the car for the three-hour drive. He helped me confess every sin He brought before me. I was a different person when I walked into the door of the house. But I couldn't speak to my wife for a week. Then Satan

155

came and tried to make me doubt the experience. Had God really spoken to me? I went into deep depression. I cried a lot, and for five days stayed in bed throughout the day.

"Because of the turmoil inside, over and over I said, 'Lord give me peace; Lord give me peace.' Finally, on Friday morning, I opened my wife's Bible. It had been years since I had opened a Bible.

"The first verse I saw was Luke 19:41. God seemed to say, 'If you only knew what will bring you peace—but now it is hidden from your eyes. The day will come when your enemies will build an embankment against you, and encircle you, and hem you in on every side. They will dash you to the ground, you and your children; they will not leave one stone upon another, because you did not recognize the time of God's command to you.' I immediately knew, with a profound regret, that the Lord had spoken to me: with an explanation, a warning, and a second chance. I said, 'Lord, thank you! Now I know it was you. I believe!'

"And a peace, like that when a raging sea became a calm after Jesus said, 'Be still....' came in an instant."

"Following that moment, God gave me a great desire to read the Bible. As I finished one book, He would direct me to another. That Sunday three weeks ago, I went to Sunday School and church for the first time in years."

Now, as Hermann shared his story, I knew what I had already guessed, that he was a new creature in Christ when he first walked in the door.

"When I was seeking peace from God, I couldn't

tell Wilmien what had happened. It had been almost two weeks since Dothan before I could bring myself to talk to her. I knew I needed to, but I couldn't bring myself to tell her. At eleven o'clock one night I told her to sit on the bed, and I shared the whole experience. 'The Lord also told me to commit myself to you one hundred percent,' I told her.

"We went to see Brother Eddie. During our discussion, we decided to renew our marriage vows before the church. Wilmien thought it would be a witness to other couples."

It was indeed a witness. There were few dry eyes in the house when the service was over. Brother Eddie asked both Hermann and Wilmien to share their testimonies. Hermann shared the story he had told me, including his walk away from God when he was about nineteen or twenty. God used Wilmien's testimony to speak to married couples.

"I didn't become a Christian until just before we were married. Hermann liked me the way I was before. But we got married anyway. After I accepted Christ, and throughout over ten years of marriage, our lives became almost unmanageable. We moved a lot and most times I never bothered to unpack all the boxes because I thought we might not stay together. My parents worried about me when we came to the USA. They were afraid we might break up and I would be left alone in a foreign country with no one to look after me.

"When Hermann told me what had happened to him in Dothan, I knew God had answered my prayers."

157

After their testimonies, they requested that Brother Eddie and I lay hands on them and pray as they knelt at the alter. Couples in the congregation were invited to come and be a part of their commitment to each other. The Holy Spirit moved that day as a formerly strife-torn family became one in Christ.

Most people didn't know about the friction that had been in the family before God revealed Himself to Hermann. Like many couples who are at odds with each other, they camouflaged it pretty well in public. But six-year-old Carl had told Rachel when he and his daddy first visited, "I feel bad when my mama and daddy fight."

Hermann's and Wilmien's renewal was the miracle beginning of a new family ready to begin their walk in the center of the Master's will. Hermann didn't know it, but already God was using him as he shared.

That same day Jeff Newton was attending Camden Baptist Church for the first time. Later Jeff said, "Like Hermann, I too was the son of a minister. I loved my dad, but I couldn't tell him my deepest feelings. I got involved with things that led me away from God. Then I heard Hermann talking about how the Lord came to him. God spoke to me through his testimony. I thought about it all afternoon. I attended church again that Sunday night and went forward during the invitation. I was thinking in terms of re-dedication. But as I talked to Brother Eddie, I came to realize I had never really met Jesus. He prayed with me and I received Christ."

Again, Hermann and Wilmien talked with Brother Eddie. They wanted to be baptized and join the church fellowship. Jeff also wanted baptism, but he wanted his dad to do it. On the appointed evening, Eddie asked Hermann, Wilmien and Jeff to give their testimonies before the baptism service. Eddie gave an invitation for others to come when they finished. Jeff's wife, Melanie, came forward. Like Jeff, she had not really met Jesus. She wanted to be baptized with her husband but had no extra clothes. A choir robe was suggested but she didn't want that.

The congregation, not aware of what was going on in Eddie's office, sang songs while God made preparations for the baptismal service. He spoke to Betty Henderson who has a ladies clothing store. "You have clothes in your van. Get an outfit for Melanie to use for baptism."

The preacher's wife, Babs, who usually brings the right number of towels, had already brought an extra, not knowing the reason.

The auditorium was darkened and the ceremony took place by candlelight. God was there that night as two couples, destined for service in His kingdom, were raised to newness of life.

Only time will tell what God will do in the lives of the two couples. Hermann came from a musical family and could play a guitar. After his conversion, he brought the guitar and sang "Great is Thy Faithfulness" during a special in church. While praising the Lord and thanking Him for His undeserving love and mercy, tears came to his eyes. The Lord then led him to lead the singing prior to

159

the Wednesday night prayer meetings.

The whole church has been touched by Hermann's genuine sincerity which is expressed when someone has been with Jesus. For example, Bill Albritton, one of Hermann's fellow Sunday School members, was deeply impressed by the Holy Spirit as he saw God working in Hermann's life. This led Bill to go away to a family mountain cabin for a solitary two-day retreat. He came back praising God for a new closeness in his life.

"I have told the Lord, I'll do what He wants me to do. It's in his hands," said Hermann. Wilmien has made the same commitment.

Jeff, who can't be at church every Sunday because he works on a rotating shift, has become part of a Sunday devotional group at work. Already he has helped a co-worker make a new commitment.

This story has been about new beginnings. Be assured, that what God starts, He will surely finish. Also be assured that everyone has a chance to know Jesus in a personal way. Just listen and be obedient when He calls.

Hermann and Wilmien have both accepted God's call into full-time Christian work. Hermann felt God's leadership to attend the Southern Baptist Seminary in Canada. However his application for a student visa was delayed and he was unable to enroll for the fall semester of 1997. In the meantime, he is a frequent speaker in area churches. He and Wilmien are teaching a singles Sunday school class while they wait for the Lord to open the next door.

22

I Think My Transmission Went out for a Reason

That if thou shalt confess with thy mouth the Lord Jesus, and shalt believe in thine heart that God hath raised him from the dead, thou shalt be saved. For with the heart man believeth unto righteousness; and with the mouth confession is made unto salvation. For whosoever shall call upon the name of the Lord shall be saved. (Romans 10:9, 10, 13)

All day she sat in David Russell's favorite booth reading the book. Other customers came and went, but she didn't seem to notice.

She had been glued to the spot, and the book, since two preachers brought her to Stuckey's gift and snack store shortly after it opened on the

163

morning of January 10, 1997. On their way to a funeral, the ministers had given the Arden, North Carolina girl a ride as she stood by her disabled car. Arriving at the store, she first called her parents to come get her. Then she asked if she could read the book, a title she had noticed in the store when she happened to stop on her way to Louisiana, more than a month before. She thought it was unusual that her car broke down at almost the same spot she had already visited.

By 3:30 that afternoon, she was nearing the end of *GOD, IF YOU'RE REAL, LET THE COW BE IN THE PEN WHEN I GET HOME.* Bert Russell, Manager of the Stuckey's store had spoken to Carrie McKinney when she first arrived and knew her situation. She stopped reading as he was about to take his girls for piano practice.

"Mr. Russell, as I have been reading this book, I have decided that my transmission went out for a reason. Maybe I am supposed to be here."

About 4:00 o'clock Bert took the girls for the piano lesson. He later commented, "On the way, the Lord spoke to me, 'I brought her here for you to tell her about me.'

"At first I argued with God. I hadn't planned to go back to the store right away. God spoke again, 'I thought you wanted to help wayward girls. Carrie has already told you she went to Louisiana to escape personal problems. When she decided she couldn't run away, she started home. I brought her here for you to help.' God had said enough. I literally ran to the booth when I got to the store. Carrie had just finished the book when I sat down."

164

"I really believe God brought me here for a reason," said Carrie.

"Just like many of the stories in the book, Jesus wants to come into your life and save you. He wants to make a new person out of you. He wants to give you a good life here on earth, and to give you eternal life in heaven," shared Bert.

"That's what I want·but I am not sure I know what to do," answered Carrie.

"If you believe you are a sinner, and are sorry for your sins, you can ask Jesus to forgive you, if you truly believe He died on the cross to redeem you. I will pray with you and lead you in the sinner's prayer," explained Bert.

Without regard to other people in the store, Carrie became our sister in Christ. She and Bert talked about the next step—finding a Bible believing church and asking for believer's baptism.

"You can't grow in Christ without spending time reading the Bible," emphasized Bert.

"I have tried to read the Bible, but it never had much meaning," admitted Carrie.

"Take your glasses off and read this to me," said Bert.

"I can't see the fine print without my glasses," responded Carrie

When Carrie put her glasses back on and said she could see again, Bert said, "That's the way it is now that you are a Christian. God will reveal His word to you, and you will now be able to understand."

Bert related that as they continued to rejoice in Carrie's victory, her parents arrived.

Carrie's first words were, "I can't wait to tell you what happened to me today."

As Bert and his wife, Lynn, related the story to me, Bert said, "When we gave Carrie the book and watched her leave with her parents, she beamed like the brightness of a 250 watt light. That morning when she arrived she looked like someone in a dark room with only a 50 watt bulb."

But the story didn't end when Carrie left Alabama. A week later she called Bert and began to quote Scripture. "I have meaningful verses on the refrigerator door and throughout the house. God has really been opening His word to me. Bert, I want you to pray for my mother and dad. When I told them what happened to me, they didn't seem to understand. My grandmother was the same way when I told her."

A week later she called again. "Keep on praying, my mother is asking questions. I think God is beginning to deal with her. Praise God! I think I found the church He wants me to attend."

I expect there is going to be much more to this story, but this is where it was when I stopped at Stuckey's on my way to Rock Springs Baptist Church last Saturday, February 1, 1997. On a previous passing, I had left some books with them for sale in their gift shop. Lynn greeted me first, "We sold two of the books and gave one away." Then Bert came in, and with great joy related the above story.

God had done with Carrie what He planned to do that day. He had used a broken transmission; two ministers accompanied by a deputy sheriff; a book; and a man on call, along with his wife Lynn, to bring a 23-year-old young lady into His Kingdom. The Bible says the trees clap their hands every time this happens. I believe there might have been an angel also involved. After all, it did take place in David Russell's favorite booth.

David Russell, Bert's father, was a foreign missionary who served in Peru, South America for twenty-six years. When he was home on furlough, he walked out to the mailbox in front of the store to get the mail, and was gunned down in a drive-by shooting. He survived, but never fully recovered. He often came to the store, but was never able to do much. So he spent a lot of hours in his special booth talking to friends or reading. I read his story in the papers and stopped to meet him. We had a long conversation about he and his wife's work on the mission field.

His health slowly declined and he lost his purpose for living. The last time I saw him he said, "I wish I had died when I was shot."

A year ago this past January, he went home to be with the Lord.

When I met Bert in November, I commented about his father, "I can't understand why God would allow one of his faithful servants to come to such an untimely end. Although I expect He has a purpose, I sure don't understand it."

"I'm the purpose," said Bert. "I don't think I would have ever gotten my life straightened out, if I had not had to watch my father slowly drift away."

Although saved at eleven, Bert made a new

commitment to serve the Lord and became active in the Pintlalla Baptist Church. After that decision, he and Lynn felt called to build a home for wayward girls.

When I asked him if that was his vision, he said, "It's more than a vision. We already have the land and most of the money."

The long drive to Chambers County was shorter as I thought about how big God is. Nothing short of His miraculous power could bring to reality the story I had just heard. Back home at church on Wednesday night, I told Brother Eddie and Hermann, "God's giving me one chapter at a time to write. I wonder what He'll give me next."

23

Pecan Buyer or Jesus Disciple?

He first findeth his own brother Simon, and saith unto him, we have found the Messiah, which is, being interpreted the Christ. And he brought him to Jesus ----.
(John 1:41-42)

The rain, which started the day before, continued throughout the night and into the day. I tried to utilize the morning by doing some writing but by noontime I wanted to get outside. I'm an outside person by day. I do most of my writing at night—usually late at night.

By 3:00 P.M., I was getting cabin fever. Then the rain stopped. I went outside and checked the rain gauge. Two inches of water was standing everywhere. It was a good time to do some maintenance work on my tractor. I had barely started when a car drove into the yard. I immediately recognized the driver. "Do you still have any pecans?" asked Fleet as he got out of the car.

Fleet was an elderly gentleman who had spent his working days as a service mechanic at a local station. He had been retired for a few years when I first met him. I noticed he had someone with him, as he usually did when he visited. "This is Charles. He rode out with me," said Fleet.

I explained to Fleet that we took most of the pecans we had left after the Christmas holidays to a shelling plant in Troy; but I did keep a few. "How many do you want?"

I knew Fleet's answer before he told me. He never bought more than five pounds at a time. But he made a lot of trips, and he always brought someone different with him. We soon had his five pounds weighed.

"Fleet, do you think Charles needs a set of the Magic Cards?" I asked as he was putting the pecans in his car.

"I 'spect he does," smiled Fleet.

Charles, like most visitors, was a ready participant and I soon told him he was 34 years old. Then came the question about eternal life. Charles didn't know about eternal life, but he was quick to say that he wanted to know. I read the Bible verses on the back of the cards and shared my testimony. I knew Charles was ready to accept Jesus before I gave the invitation. After he said yes, I explained about every knee bowing and acknowledging that Jesus is Lord.

"I'll get some grape box lids so we can bow our knees to the Lord and have our prayer on the wet ground."

Charles, Fleet, and I kneeled on the box lids and Christ became real in Charles' life. When we had finished praying, I told Charles I wanted to ask him a question. "Has God been dealing with you before today? Have you been thinking about Him lately?"

"Yes I have been thinking about getting my life straight with the Lord for a while," admitted Charles.

"I thought so. I can usually tell when someone is being drawn by the Holy Spirit to Christ. He just sent you out here with Fleet for me to tell you how to come to Him."

Before they left, we talked about church, baptism, and following Jesus. Fleet promised to see me again.

After they were gone, a thought came to my mind, "I believe this happened before. Didn't someone else Fleet brought here make a decision for Christ?"

Later, when I shared the experience with Rachel, I said, "You know what I believe? I believe Fleet is bringing all these different people to me so I can tell them about Jesus. He always seems to take a big interest when I share. He may not be interested in buying pecans as much as he is in helping them learn about Jesus."

24

Peer Pressure and the Stolen Pipe

-- follow not that which is evil, but that which is good. He that doeth good is of God: but he that doeth evil hath not seen God. (III John 1:11)

Laura McClain, a senior at Wilcox Academy in charge of the weekly chapel devotion, asked me to be their speaker on March 3, 1997. I knew it would be quite demanding—keeping the attention of the whole student body from grades kindergarten through twelve. But I knew it was payback time. God had blessed and taken care of me in my school years when I could have faltered badly without His help.

From the beginning, when Laura first asked me to do the program, I knew God wanted me to talk about peer pressure. I also knew I must write a long overdue letter before I could give the program. It would be a time of swallowing some pride, and making a confession, if the Lord's message was going to be meaningful to the children. It was a time of mixed emotions, intermingled with a lot of prayer, as I asked God to prepare my thoughts for the program.

March the third was like a spring day when I arrived at the school. Laura met me outside the gym. "I'm just enjoying the sun after all the rainy weather we've been having," was her greeting.

We talked about her college plans which were still uncertain. Several months earlier she had made a commitment to serve the Lord in whatever direction He led. Laura had become one of my favorite people as I watched her develop in our church youth group. For two years she had worked to raise funds for summer mission trips, first to Central America, and this past summer, Russia. As we talked about her travels and future plans, I thought of how different my high school years were. She had already been, and would probably go to other places, to tell people about Jesus. In my case, I knew when I finished high school, I would be traveling to some far away places too, but for a very different reason—World War II was raging throughout the world.

The 350 students filed into the gym and filled the bleachers. Buddy Sumner, the headmaster, told me the school had a chapel program each week, organized by the students. After Laura made her introduction, I told the students I was going to talk about some of the things I remembered about my youth, and the peer pressure I experienced when I was in school.

"Does peer pressure ever make you do anything you don't want to do?

"I want to share some experiences I had in school when I listened to the beat of the wrong drummer. It's not going to be easy for me to do this, but I am hoping it will help you. There is a verse in the Bible which highlights what I want to say. It's found in 3 John 1:11. Let me read it.

'*Follow not that which is evil, but that which is good. He that doeth good is of God: but he that doeth evil hath not seen God.*'

"Before I talk to you older people about peer pressure, let me first say a few words to our young folks," I said as I directed my attention to the lower grades.

I asked those in the first, second, and third grades to hold up their hands. "I was about your age when I prayed about our milk cow coming home. I played with my neighbor until late that evening, rather than find our cow and drive her home so we could have fresh milk. When it began to get dark, I didn't want to go into the woods and hunt her because I was afraid the panther might get me. My daddy had shot at the panther and it probably left the country. But when dark came, I thought it might still be out there, so I went home without the cow.

"Have any of you ever failed to do something your daddy or mama wanted you to do? Did you feel bad because you forgot to do it?" Several young hands went up when I asked the questions.

I knew they were with me.

"I felt bad because we wouldn't have any milk. I had heard adults say, if we pray about something, God would hear our prayer. I wondered if God would hear my prayer if I asked Him to let the cow be in the pen when I got home. I decided to ask. And you know what? She was! I don't think God will answer a prayer like that every time; because we are supposed to do what our mama and daddy tell us. I think He answered my prayer to show me He is real, that He loves us and wants to give us good things. He wants to give us eternal life so we can be with Him forever. Many of you have already asked Him to come into your heart. I waited a long time before I asked Him to come into mine.

"I had finished school and became a seaman. In the middle of the Atlantic Ocean our ship was caught in a storm. We were carrying a load of coal and the coal caught fire. We thought we would sink. I knew if the ship did sink and I drowned, I wouldn't go to heaven because I hadn't asked Jesus to save me. But that day I did ask Him to come into my heart and forgive my sins. He did and now I can go to heaven. If you haven't asked Him into your heart yet, don't wait a long time like I did."

Next I asked the fourth and fifth grade to hold up their hands. I then told a story about peer pressure which happened to me when I was their age. Spending the night with me was a classmate whose father had been killed in an accident when he was small. When we went to the store for mama, he asked if I had any money. I had a paper route so I did have some change. He wanted me to buy a package of ready roll "Wing" cigarettes, which cost a dime in those days. I didn't want to buy the cigarettes because my folks had told me never to smoke.

"I'll buy them but you don't have to tell anyone," he said.

I didn't want to smoke but because he insisted, I gave him the dime. But my Aunt Ada saw us smoking and told my parents. I'll never forget the confrontation they had with me the next night. I felt awful because I had violated their trust. My first cousin, Teddy Cooper, made it even worse the next day when he said, "Ick, (my nick-name) I didn't think you would do something like that." Teddy was a year older than me and I give him a lot of credit for helping make the adjustment in later school years from Rosinton to Robertsdale High. He promoted "good" peer pressure and I shall always be grateful. Families stuck together in those days. If a member got out of line, he or she could expect discipline from other members. If we do things which bring dishonor, the whole family suffers. Everything we do affects our family name."

I next diverted my attention to the high school section. "Like many of you, I played all sports in high school, partly because of the encouragement of Teddy. Teddy loved football. He read every book about the game he could find. He became the starting quarterback when he was in the ninth grade. During his career, he led the school to some of its most victorious years. I was in the eleventh grade before I made the starting team. It was to

Teddy's credit that we jelled into a winning team, losing only to Pensacola High, a much larger school. From his quarterback position, Teddy saw everything that happened on the field. "Ick, you missed your man that play. You can handle him," were his typical encouraging words. Because he believed in us, we were over-achievers and usually beat our opponents by four or five touchdowns. Teddy promoted good peer pressure, both on and off the field.

"My senior year was very different. Sometimes we listen to a different drummer. In fall football practice, a fad was started among the team. Everybody was supposed to get a tobacco pipe. There was one catch! We couldn't buy it, we were to steal it.

"I wasn't the best ball player on the team. But I did have enough leadership ability to have squelched the fad when I was told about it.

"I could have confronted the player who told me, and reminded him of the goals we should have had for a winning team—which sure didn't include smoking pipes and certainly not stealing. But I didn't.

"I thought I needed to belong to the group. I didn't realize I could be part of a much better group by taking a stand against something not right.

"After practice we usually went to the local drug store for refreshments. In the back of the store was a couple of display aisles. A cardboard holding several pipes was on one rack. When no one was looking, I removed a pipe and put it in my pocket. But just as this happened, one of my classmates, who worked in the drug store after school, walked down the other aisle and saw my action. I don't know if he knew about the fad or not. He didn't say anything. Maybe he thought I was going to pay for it. But I didn't pay and it has haunted me every since.

"Several years later, I went back to Robertsdale with the intention of paying for the $1.25 pipe, plus interest. I was told the former owners were deceased.

"I've told you this story because I thought it might help you handle wrong peer pressure. You just won a state football championship against a lot of odds. Those of you who play football already know what good peer pressure is. There were some good peer leaders on your team. You would not have won a championship without good leaders. If I asked each of you to write the names of three teammates who encouraged you to give your best performance, I expect the same three names would be on most papers. If I asked the coaches to do the same, the names might be different. Real leaders on the field of battle are not always the ones heard on the sidelines. They just give their best and are not looking for self-glory. That's what I want to encourage each of you to do. Be the kind of peer leader who stands for the right things in life.

"There's a billboard sign at the foot of the hill coming into Camden. It has a picture of a pretty young girl, with a teasing expression, holding a cigarette. The caption reads, 'Misty-Light 'n Sassy.' The tobacco company is directing the ad to young people like you. In their subtle way they are saying, 'This is the way, smoke and have fun.' They don't care if smoking will cause you to have cancer; or emphysema; or shorten your life by years; or cause someone else the same misery by second hand smoke. All they want is to get you addicted to tobacco. Then the chances are they will get your money for the rest of your life. Too, they know if they get only a few of you through their sign, they can get many more of you through peer pressure—if they get those of you who are leaders. Don't let them make you that kind of peer leader.

"If I knew all of you well, I could pick out some excellent peers. I know there are a lot of good ones in this student body. But I do want to recognize Laura as being someone we can all admire. If you haven't read her essay about citizenship, you need to find a copy and read it. It was printed in *The Progressive Era* last week. She has a challenge for all of us of every age. "Laura, I am proud of you."

"Now let me tell you about the letter I had to write before I could speak to you. As I said before, it wasn't easy for me to confess to you about stealing the pipe. I wanted to make amends but the former store owners are gone. So the Lord directed me to write a letter to my classmate, apologize to him, and make my confession to you.

"I wrote the letter about ten days ago. My classmate's name is Harry Wilters. He's a Circuit Judge and has a responsible job as he deals with many people. In my letter, I reviewed everything that happened. Since he saw me take the pipe, I asked his forgiveness. I enclosed a hundred dollars, for the pipe and interest, and asked him to help me make amends by using the money to help some young person who was marching to a different drummer.

"I hope none of you will listen to the wrong peer people as I did. I hope you will never have to write a letter to make amends because you made a wrong choice."

25

I'm Slow to Learn Obedience

Obey my voice, and I will be your God, and ye shall be my people: and walk ye in all the ways I have commanded you, that it may be well unto you. (Jeremiah 7:23)

It hardly seemed possible that it had been eighteen years since the timber had been harvested and replanted on our land near Suttle in Perry County. Bill Grimes, a MacMillan Bloedel forester in charge of managing the land, had called and said they were starting a thinning harvest. I was on my way to move our hunting tree stands so they wouldn't be broken during the harvest. As I passed through Camden, the Holy Spirit impressed me that it was time to stop and witness to Larry.

I'd known Larry for a few years. He worked in

a store that bought my muscadines. Like most people I dealt with in the muscadine trade, I had given Larry a set of the magic cards. Recently I had stopped in the store to pick up a take out lunch at their deli. It was past the rush hour so I was about to give a set of cards to the server when Larry walked up. As Larry watched, I played the game with the lady and asked the question about eternal life! But just as I asked the question, another customer came and she turned her attention to him. As she did so, I directed my discussion to Larry.

"I don't remember how you answered the question about eternal life, Larry. Do you know if you died you would go to heaven?"

Larry made a sheepish smile and said he didn't know. I didn't feel this was the time or the place for me to continue the witness. The other customer quickly left and I said to the server, "If you already know about eternal life, get familiar with the Bible verses on the back and share them with your friends who don't know. However, if you still have a question, maybe they will help you," I said as I explained how the numbers game worked.

"Larry, I'll get back with you and we'll talk some more about eternal life," were my parting words.

Twice I tried to see Larry. One day I detoured through town to talk with him. Both times he was not working. Now the Lord was telling me to stop when I had a very busy day planned. But I have already learned that the Lord's ways are not our ways. Yet, with my full day planned, was this really the Spirit telling me to take the time to visit?

I already had one planned stop in Camden

before the sixty-mile drive to Suttle. On the previous Friday, I had bought some onion plants at the Wilcox Farm Center. They were stuck together like one bundle; but when I planted them I realized I had two bundles. I wasn't sure Mrs. Jackson charged me for the two bunches so I wanted to get it straight. She remembered my purchase and I hadn't paid for two bunches.

I got back into my truck and prayed, "God, do you want me to go back and see Larry today? Can I do it another day? You know about the tractor parts I need to find in Selma; and I need to see the loggers and move the tree stands. It's going to be a full day if I'm going to get back in time for church."

How do you describe a pleading child who wants to do something different from what a parent wants? Or a parent who finally consents to letting the child do what he wants? I guess that's the way I felt as I drove away toward Selma.

God gave me a good day. I had a sharing time with three men at a tractor dealership. A store that sells our muscadines agreed to sell the raccoons I had caught around the vineyard. Keeping varmints out of the vineyard is an on-going job. However, I don't believe the animals should be killed and wasted. I believe God created them for man's use so I dressed and froze them so they wouldn't be wasted.

I arrived at the logging site just as the men were breaking for lunch. It was the perfect time to share the "Magic Cards" and talk about Jesus. After eating lunch and resting a while at the camp house, I still had time to go fishing in the pond. The pond has always been productive. We can usually catch a mess of fish. But for some reason, maybe not being there to add enough fertilize, we never catch large bass. But that afternoon I caught the largest one yet, a six-and-a-half pounder. I got home just in time to make church.

Bill Bright, founder of Campus Crusade For Christ, has commented that he evaluates what he has done toward carrying out the "Great Commission" at the close of each day. I sometimes try to do that. When I read my Bible before bedtime that Wednesday night, I knew I had missed something the Lord wanted me do that day. "Lord, give me another chance," was my prayer. Neither was that my last prayer as I thought about my disobedience throughout the week.

The next Wednesday morning I decided it was time to go check on the loggers again. Too, I wanted to see if the wild turkeys were still on the place after all the logging activity. I hated that the logging came almost at the start of turkey season. Steve and I had planted a large patch of chuffa, hoping they would hold the turkeys for the spring hunting season.

Activity was just beginning in Camden when I drove through town. Then came the unmistakable small voice, "Now is the time to see Larry."

For a fleeing moment, I thought about the raccoons which might thaw out if I delayed. But it didn't matter!   I wasn't going to miss my assignment a second time.

There was hardly a customer in the store when I entered. Larry was alone in a corner, putting up stock. After our greetings, I said, "Larry, the last time we talked you told me you didn't know about eternal life. I tried to see you a couple of times since but you weren't here. Last week, I felt I should have come but didn't. Let me ask you, has God been dealing with you lately? Have you been thinking about Him?"

Larry, usually having a perpetual smile, made a slight, sincere grin, as he said, "yes."

"I thought so because God has been directing me back to you after we talked before. Let me explain what we have to do to make things right with God so we can be saved."

Larry and I stepped into a back storeroom so we wouldn't be disturbed. In a few minutes, without hesitation, he and I got on our knees and he asked Jesus into his life. It was one of the easiest presentations of the plan of salvation I have ever made. God had prepared Larry and he only needed to be told how to come.

As I drove toward Selma, I thought about how unimportant the things of this world are compared to a man's soul.

26

The Vision

And David said to Joab and to the rulers of the people, Go, number Israel from Beersheba even to Dan; and bring the number of them to me, that I may know it.

And Joab answered, the Lord make his people an hundred times as many more as they are; but, my lord the king, are they not all my lord's servants? Why, then, doth my lord require this thing? Why will he be a cause of trespass to Israel? (I Chronicles 21:2-3)

This passage about David's life has troubled me. When David asked Joab to make a census, why did God, through His angel, bring pestilence upon the land and kill seventy thousand men? I have heard preachers give sermons about the numbering, but I didn't have a clear answer until I read the story again a few days ago. Not only did the Scripture help me see David's position but it also helped me understand my own.

My understanding came through my catfish fingerling project. I believe that is the way God often deals with us—through our day-to-day activities. We started raising catfish in the early seventies when the enterprise was just beginning. Finding the baby catfish was sometimes difficult so we decided to consider raising our own fingerlings.

When we first decided to build the big lake and go into the catfish business, we selected a house site which would overlook the horseshoe-shaped lake. To get to the house site, we had to build a road across a boggy hollow.

We tried to cross the hollow at one location, but the site had no foundation. When we moved the crossing downstream, we realized the roadway could serve as a dam for another small pond. However, we couldn't clear the wet site very well with a conventional crawler tractor. We did raise one crop of catfish in the lake, then the idea of making it into a brood pond came. But the site would have to be cleared better for seining fingerlings. Clearing could only be done by a drag line. It would be expensive to bring in a contractor. We would have to borrow the money. Would the investment pay its way? Too, I didn't know how to raise fingerlings. Could it be done nature's way without building a hatchery? I read what little information was available and pondered these questions in my mind for several days.

One day as I was praying about the project, God gave me a very clear answer through a vision. Some people question the reality of God speaking to us through visions. Long ago, I decided it best not to talk about visions, especially to unbelievers. But I know what I saw, and I believe God was in it. The resulting years have confirmed that belief. Furthermore, the Bible has stories of God speaking through visions. While I was praying, the vision came. I saw a large yellow machine on the edge of the pond bank. It had a long boom with a bucket attachment reaching out clearing the brush and muck. It was God's answer to bring in Mr. Bennett, the road-building contractor I had been talking to who had been working in the area. His equipment operator was Ed Poole, the same man I had bought the place from who then lived near Montgomery. With the bucket, mounted on the long boom, he worked around the pond, digging out the stumps and mud. Within a few days, he had it ready for raising fingerlings.

I found some hollow logs, cut them into three-foot lengths, nailed a board across one end, then staked them down around the edges of the pond. I surmised that this was nature's way of raising catfish in the wild. I selected the best looking fish for the brooders when we sold fish crops. Not only did we produce enough fingerlings for restocking the grow-out pond each year but also usually had a surplus to sell.

Some years we made more money from the surplus fingerlings than we did the grow-out pond. In addition we saved the cost of buying stockers.

Steve and Diane were getting their family started and like most young couples sometimes struggled financially. I offered him a partnership for selling fingerlings in Coosa County. He sold several thousand, which helped him and us. The pond literally turned to fingerlings in the formative years. As the pond got older, production declined; but we usually had plenty for restocking, and some surplus.

Raising fingerlings has been hard work, but there have also been other rewards. Each year we must drain the pond, put the brood fish in a holding area, remove all wild fish which will eat the eggs, and let the pond refill with new water, then return the brood fish. The reward comes when I see the first fry after the spawning season as I place feed around the submerged logs. I can spend hours watching the schools of thousands of young fish move to and fro. When this happens, you know that your work has not been in vain, and God has blessed with a new crop.

Now back to this year and David's story of numbering the people. I have already written about cutting back on catfish production in the grow-out pond, so we plan to sell most of this year's crop of fingerlings. However, the buyers have been slow to call. My name is on a state list of fingerling producers. In almost twenty-five years of raising fingerlings, I have never done any advertising. People wanting fingerlings have always matched production. As I thought about the slow response this year, I considered doing some advertising. More than once, I thought about composing an ad and sending it to area newspapers. Then I read the numbering story, first in 2 Samuel 24 and a few days later in I Chronicles 21.

God had blessed David all the days of his life. He was "a man after God's own heart." But David quit trusting God when he wanted to know how many fighting men he had. Without God, a million and three hundred thousand would not be enough to keep his enemies from over running him. But to David's credit, he always confessed his sins when made aware of them. God stopped the death angel from destroying Jerusalem when he confessed.

That's how God spoke to me through David's story. Had He not always sent buyers for the fingerlings? Had He not always sold the food fish when they were ready? Was I going to take matters in my own hands and sell the fingerlings through advertising when He had always done it?

I made a commitment, "Lord, you can sell them or they can stay in the pond. I'm trusting you to do whatever you will with them."

The next day I got two phone calls. Although not large orders, both wanted fingerlings. I don't even know how many I have. I never know for sure until they are seined. Whatever we have, I believe God will do something with them.

I will add that I don't believe there is anything wrong with advertising. I just think it would not have been trusting God in my case about the fish. After all, He's the one who put me into the fish business and gave me the vision about the fingerlings.

27

Back to My Roots

And let us arise, and go up to Bethel; and I will make there an altar unto God, who answered me in the day of my distress, and was with me in the way which I went. (Genesis 35:3)

My sister, Jeanette Ryan, called and said our uncle Bill had died. Burial would be in the Dyess Cemetery in Rosinton, Alabama. I told Jeanette I planned to come and pay my last respects to our 91-year-old uncle. The trip would mean going back to my roots.

When I was growing up, I could almost see the cemetery from our house. I spent a lot of hours browsing through the old church and cemetery. My great-grandfather, Winfield Scott Dyess, and my grandfather, Elijah Louis Dyess, were buried there, along with my grandmother and other relatives and neighbors. Both grandparents had died before I was born.

As I drove to Baldwin County on the morning of April 21, 1997, my thoughts went back again to my youth. They had been good years. A highlight of my youth was the one-acre okra patch Daddy had helped me clear and plant for my 4-H project. Mr. Johnson, my 4-H club advisor, had featured my name in a news article as the only member in the whole county who had okra for a project that year. Sometimes the okra would make my fingers bleed before picking was finished but the money it brought helped the family through some hard times.

I remembered Bernard and myself building a little miniature bridge out of pine poles, so we could walk across a wet weather stream between our house and the field. The bridge didn't last long but it was an engineering feat for my young years. It was in that same creek bottom where we had the excitement each fall of finding chincapins which grew along the hollow. We always watched for the first burrs to open so we could beat the squirrels to the tasty nuts. Then the chestnut blight came and wiped out not only one of America's choice native trees but also its near kin, the chincapin.

I also remembered my first experience with death, when my Uncle George had died at a young age. I was ten. The picture of tears in the eyes of my five cousins, as they sat in a car near the grave side, is still fresh in my memory.

As I grew, I visited the cemetery often. I knew the names on every tombstone. I wondered about their lives as I figured how long they had lived.

Thinking about them made me consider my own place in eternity. Now, two days after God had given me my three score and ten years, I was going back to the cemetery again.

I stopped in Frisco City to get gas. "God, if you have someone for me to witness to, keep other customers away and make the opportunity." A man was leaving as I paid for my gas. I didn't see anyone else inside.

"Would you like to have a set of my Magic Cards?" I asked the young clerk as she handed my change.

"Magic cards?" was her quizzical answer.

"Yes, these cards can tell me how old you are if you don't mind me knowing." She didn't mind and in a few seconds I told her she was twenty-one.

"How did you do that?" was her quick question.

I showed her the system, then turned to the back and the question about eternal life. She hesitated for a moment, then said she didn't know about eternal life. I said a silent prayer and asked God again to keep others away. As I went through the Bible verses, I could see the Holy Spirit working as her eyes became misty. I noticed a car drive to the gas pumps. I knew I had to hurry. I told her how I became a Christian at sea. "You can have Jesus anytime you really want Him. Just surrender your life to His Lordship."

The new customer came into the building. I asked about the location of the rest room. When I was returning to my car, I saw the young lady looking at the cards. She wasn't looking at the numbers game as many people do when they first get the cards. She was reading the Bible verses again. I knew God had spoken.

As I continued my drive on the late spring morning, I thought about today's youth and their life compared to mine. Many of my generation wanted to give their children more than we had. Maybe in so doing, we have robbed them of something far more valuable. Have we tried to make adults out of them too early? Have we tried to give them the best at the expense of waiting and earning the right to be an adult? For example, I remember family gatherings for special occasions. There was never enough seating space when meal-time came. We ate by first table, second table, third table, etc. Children didn't eat first like they might today. We ate after all the adults had eaten. If the choice pieces of chicken were gone, we understood. We would get the privilege of eating at the first table when we became adults. When I asked why I had to do something, they might give me a reason. But there were times when I might hear, "Because I said so." Today, some say that's not a good answer. But it was with me because I knew they knew more than I did. I'd just have to wait until I got older to get the answers.

I've heard as we get older we tend to remember the good and forget the bad. That's probably true. But I still remember a lot of the bad. Children branded each other in my day, just as they do today. We even put each other into three social classes relating to the lunch we carried in a new syrup bucket before the day of school lunchrooms. If your parents could afford 'light bread' for your sandwiches, you belonged to the elite class. If your sandwich was made with biscuits, you were middle class. If all you had was fried corn bread, even if it had a slice of home cured ham between, you were on the bottom, and might be called a "corn bread eater." Most of the time we had biscuits but sometimes we didn't. On those days mama would fry those golden brown fritters for my sandwiches. But mine never got to school. On the way, I hid my syrup bucket in the woods and did without lunch that day. It tasted mighty good that afternoon on the way home, but I wasn't about to be called a "corn bread eater."

But there were some things you couldn't hide on the way to school. Although Mama tried very hard to bleach out the lettering, there might still be the dim imprint of the 6-8-4 fertilizer number on my homemade shirt. Most of the time she could cut out the shirt in a way that the bib of my overalls would hide the number. I've wondered why today's kids will pay huge prices for faded jeans and overalls, with the torn knee patches, and blue denim shirts with the 6-8-4 plainly imprinted. Could it be, even though they have the latest in modern clothing, they realize something is missed?

The Great Depression years of the thirties can never be understood by anyone who wasn't there. I don't remember the booming years of the Roaring Twenties, since I was not born until 1927. But two indelible memories happened in 1936-37 which crystallized the difficulty my parents endured just to keep food for the family. Daddy didn't believe in the welfare programs Franklin D. Roosevelt started.

Nevertheless, when free flour was being passed out in the communities, he and two of his brothers went to Mr. Hankins' house late one evening after work to get a sack. Mr. Hankins, the community representative, said he only had two sacks. He let them draw straws. The short straw wouldn't get any. Daddy got the short straw. He never went again, choosing to feed his family by the sweat of his brow.

A year later in 1937, the economy wasn't any better. When daddy wasn't looking after our little farm, he worked for neighbors. The going rate was fifty cents a day—all day. Fifty cents was the price of a 24-pound sack of flour—in a print cloth sack which could be used for making dresses. One afternoon when I got home from school, I was sent to the store to get a sack of flour. When I approached the storekeeper to get the flour on credit, he refused. Merchants had a hard time making ends meet, too. It was dark when Daddy got home after a hard day's work. He and I went to the store. He didn't talk as we walked the half mile. Daddy was a passive fellow and usually didn't take issue with people. But I saw a determination that night which I don't remember seeing before, or since. It wasn't threatening. Yet it was spoken in such a way, I don't think anyone could have turned him down.

All he said was, "Rel, I need a sack of flour."

"You can get it," was Rel's instant reply. Those were the only words spoken as we left the country store. Going back to my roots was bringing back a lot of memories, both the good and the bad.

I never understood why my great-grandfather gave the land for the church and cemetery on the backside of the section of land he owned, rather than nearer the road to town. Maybe in his day, there was no front or back as the land was being settled. Too, when the church was established, there were no automobiles. Horses and buggies could go most anywhere.

Cousin Betty Langham, in her memoir, wrote about her and her mother walking to the church on Saturday. "Sunday Papa would take us in the buggy. They just had church twice a month, on Saturday and Sunday. It was a small church, about twenty-four by thirty-six feet. It had all wooden window shutters, no lights and no heat. We have been there when it was freezing weather and sat for two hours for two preachers to preach. Sometimes nearly every one from church would go to one place for dinner, but the ladies never did mind. There was always a stove of baked potatoes, or potato custards made, some kind of vegetables, plenty of ham, bacon, or sausage in the smokehouse, lots of eggs, milk, butter, or fryers."

As the years passed, the church declined and then was discontinued. Only the cemetery remained. Mama decided she didn't want to be buried in the cemetery because the road was often impassable for an automobile. When she died, we honored her wishes and buried her at the Rosinton Road Cemetery. Daddy was buried beside Mama. Not so with Uncle Bill. He wanted to be with his ancestors. He and his Uncle George Jasper Dyess' son, Roy Dyess, and my Uncle George's widow,

Effie Mae, got the county to solve the problem by paving the road to the cemetery. They planted grass and kept the grounds immaculate. George Langham, a nephew of Daddy's Uncle George, took over after Roy died and Uncle Bill became disabled. Uncle Willis "Bill" Dyess rode with pride as he made the journey to his final resting place.

My brother Bernard, who now pastors a church in Florida, rode with me from Robertsdale where the Memorial service was held. It was Bernard who led Uncle Bill to the Lord while pastoring a church in Rosinton.

Uncle Bill was in his seventies when he made his decision for Christ. Bernard was called to another church in Florida before he was baptized. Bernard came back to perform the ceremony but Uncle Bill was sick. Rev. Joe Langham, then Pastor of the Rosinton Road Baptist church, did the baptizing when he was better. Brother Joe said at the service, "I've baptized a lot of people but Willis is the only one who came up out of the water shouting, 'Praise the Lord! Praise the Lord!'"

The funeral procession traveled through the center of what had been great-grandfather Winfield Scott's land. A developer recently purchased part of Grandfather Elijah's land. A new white fence fronted the road. Some of the best farm land in Baldwin County will soon be converted to house sites—my youthful memories are fast perishing. Then we turned onto my great-uncle George's land. His children and grandchildren had built homes along the way. In the background we could see Uncle George's old house, which has been the site of many Dyess family gatherings, still standing, defying time. As I looked, I remembered when we all had the measles. Our cow was dry and Uncle George and Aunt Ida gave us a pail of milk each day. When I approached the house, the children all shouted for me to stay away. They had already put the milk on a post outside the yard.

I was coming home to my roots as the funeral procession made its last turn along the tree-lined road leading to the cemetery. My okra field was now in pine trees. The hollow where my little bridge had been, and the swamp below it where the panther lived, had all been cleared and made into a huge lake. Only memories remained of our house site which was located near the shore of where the lake is now. But the graves in the cemetery were still the same, only increased by new additions.

When Pastor Joe Langham and Carl Sanders finished their last prayer at the graveside, family and friends gathered in the background shade along the chain length fence to renew long ago friendships.

Aunt Alma Cloud, one of Uncle Bill's surviving sisters who lost her husband, Earl, in 1981, was faithful to look after him in his declining years. She came to me and said, "I want to give one of your books to Willis' daughter before she goes back to Texas. Do you have one with you?"

I knew Uncle Bill had a daughter but we had never met. Aunt Alma found Willie Ruth and introduced us. She was an attractive lady with a ready smile. As we talked, I shared with her a few things I remembered about Uncle Bill.

"Although your daddy was primarily a farmer, he also was somewhat of an inventor. Before the days of chain saws, he took some old bicycle wheels, a gasoline engine, a circular saw and made the first power saw in this part of the country. When I was in college, he knew I needed some extra money. So he gave me a job helping him cut poles while I was home one summer. I didn't realize until later that he gave me half of all we made."

When I returned from the car with the book, Willie Ruth introduced her husband, Thurman Sprangler, and two of her four daughters. One of the daughters made a picture of her mother and me, then Ruth asked for my address. God reminded me to give her a set of the "Magic Cards" which include the address.

Several people were still visiting in our group, including Warren Dyess, a Baptist minister from Stapleton. "My address is on this set of cards, I call them my Magic Cards. For instance, I can use them to tell your age," I said as I turned to one of Ruth's pretty daughters.

She gave her permission and we played the game as the others watched.

After I told her age, I turned the cards over to discuss eternal life.

"We all need to know the way to heaven, because all of us must go out there in the cemetery where Uncle Bill has gone. These cards have Bible verses on them which tell the way to find eternal life. If each of you already knows the way, take the cards and help someone else get there," I said as I passed out sets. I felt God was speaking as I could see the seriousness of the moment in every face.

My younger brother, George Marion, who has his lot picked out in the beautiful quiet cemetery overlooking the lake, and I had one more stop to make before our trips home. It was the Rosinton Road cemetery where our parents are buried. It too is well kept and includes a lot of relatives and friends. After Marion and I said good bye, and I was driving back to Camden and he to Pensacola, I thought more about my roots and continuing life journey.

I thought about that late evening long ago when I stopped in that freshly plowed field and asked God about His reality. His answer crystallized my spiritual life. It wasn't just that the cow was in the pen, but the warmth of His presence that made me know.

Over the years, I have thought about that evening a thousand times. The details are still fresh in my memory. But it had been good to look at the countryside again where it happened. I felt like I had been back to my own Bethel.

ROSINTON SCHOOL HAS SERVED FOUR GENERATIONS. The author remembers the first and second grades under Mrs. Higgins who taught in the near wing. The center section had two rooms, divided with folding doors, which opened into an auditorium. Mrs. Nan Dean Cooper was his third and fourth grade teacher and Mr. George Strong was principle and taught seventh and eight grade. Mrs. Lillian Kennedy had the fifth and six grades in the far wing.

28

God Wants You to Come to Montana

Those who honor me, I will honor. (I Samuel 2:30)

"God told me to walk around the Casino each day next week, and then take the church membership around it on Sunday. If we do this, He will give us the building to convert into a church," said Pastor Andrew Goodwin as we talked by phone.

"I told God the people of Hungry Horse would think I had lost my mind if they saw me breaking a trail over a hundred inches of snow, which almost came to the roof. God, if you're sure this is what you want me to do, and I'm hearing you right, tell someone else the same message.

"Would you believe one of my church members came to me and said, 'Brother Goodwin, I believe

God wants us to march around the Casino, just as Joshua did at Jericho. Then He will give it to us.' I knew then for sure what God wanted me to do."

So went my conversation with Brother Andrew Goodwin, a Southern Baptist Home Missionary in Montana. He had called one night a couple of weeks earlier. The Bibb County, Alabama native said someone had sent a copy of my book. After giving his compliments to *GOD, IF YOU'RE REAL, LET THE COW BE IN THE PEN WHEN I GET HOME*, he startled me when he said, "God wants you to come to Hungry Horse and help us build this church."

I didn't know exactly where Montana was located, just out west somewhere. But I knew it was a long way from Camden, Alabama. Furthermore, I told Brother Goodwin that we usually worked with a lay team and I was not the coordinator. Harold Swearingen was the coordinator. I agreed to pass the request to Harold.

Brother Goodwin went on to say that Hungry Horse was near Glacier National Park. Already they had 115 inches of snow and it was still early in the winter season. "It will be next June, at the earliest, before we thaw out, so a date for the Revival should be July or August."

After Brother Goodwin's first call, I said to Rachel, "You always wanted to travel out west. Well, we've just been invited to Montana." Like me, she was full of questions, most of which I couldn't answer. We began to pray and think about the possibilities of going. We would have to be back home no later than August 15th to get ready for the muscadine harvest. But as time went on, we both felt God wanted us to go. I talked to Harold and he, too, seemed receptive to getting a small team together.

A few days later, Brother Goodwin's letter stated, "I don't know all God is up to but I believe He wants to do something special in Hungry Horse. We started this ministry as a mission two years ago. Growth has been slow; however, God is on the move. We have seen fifteen saved in the last eight weeks. We average twenty-five in Sunday School. But we have many prospects. Of the 900 population in Hungry Horse, only a small percent attend church."

Included in the letter was a picture of a small church surrounded by snow. When I called to announce that we were thinking about coming, I asked about the church.

"The picture I sent you is where we've been meeting, in the Alliance Church. God has blessed us and added to our membership. We now need a place of our own. A man who owned a bar-casino-restaurant in a good location has lost it to the bank. There is another man who wants to buy the property and continue to run it as before. The bank has given us two weeks to raise $25,000 earnest money; otherwise, they will have to sell it to him. Please pray that God will send the money." Brother Goodwin then told me about God's calling to march around the building.

I marveled at Brother Goodwin's faith. There seemed little doubt that the money would be forth coming. I shared the marching story with several people I met during the week, including our church's Wednesday night prayer meeting and my Sunday School class. The missionary hadn't asked for money, only our prayers. By Sunday night, I decided to call Hungry Horse and find out what was happening. "We don't have all the money yet. But that is the way God sometimes does. He tests our faith and waits until the last minute to answer," said Brother Goodwin.

I wasn't home when Brother Andrew called. God had exceeded the goal and sent over $27,000. They were ready to start renovating the building. By March first, they had moved in. The former dining room of the casino became the sanctuary; the dance floor, Sunday school class rooms. The bar will be an information center this summer for tourists, with free ice cream and soda. God is honoring Brother Andrew's faithfulness. For a year it was only he, his family, and Opal Lynch. By Easter Sunday, ninety people attended. In his March newsletter he said, "We baptized ten last Sunday night in a horse watering trough and have twenty more awaiting baptism after counseling." God is indeed at work in Hungry Horse.

I have a feeling this is only the beginning. There is money to be raised to pay for the building and the renovation. But what God has started, He will not quit until He is finished. I don't know what role, if any, Rachel, the team, and I, will play. But we're available to go to Montana if God wants us.

On August sixth through tenth, eight lay people

became a team to help grow the church at Hungry Horse. Barry Barrett, an American Airlines pilot from Nashville; Henry and Lois McElroy from Pell City, Alabama; Carl Howard from Pine Hill; Bill Albritton, Hermann Brandt, Rachel and myself from Camden, flew to the Glacier Park International Airport about fifteen miles from Hungry Horse. Harold had a schedule conflict develop with his job and could not go, so it fell on my lot to be the coordinator. Somehow, I had felt that was going to be my job from the beginning.

The little Rocky Mountain town of Hungry Horse is located on U. S. Highway 2, a route used by many early pioneers making their way across the continental divide. The western entrance to the fabulous Glacier Park is only a short distance from the edge of the town. Much of the town's economy is geared around summer tourists who visit the park.

But we were only part of the team God sent to Hungry Horse. A couple, Maxine and Butch Wilson, from East Texas were visiting the area and were living in their travel trailer. They met Brother Andrew and he told them about the Lay Revival. God impressed them to stay. Maxine and Butch served the role of church members and were there to help with all the visitation. Maxine, an accomplished musician, played the organ for each service. Butch, a cattle rancher, told in his testimony about the power of God in saving his mangled leg almost lost in a tractor accident, then later gaining new health after brain surgery.

The Lord also arranged for Toby Smitherman

from Randolph, Alabama to be there. Toby, an ordained minister, is a pharmacist student at Samford University. While in Montana, he had been ministering on Indian reservations and working with various churches in the Montana Association. He, too, assumed the role of local church member for the revival. His dedication was an inspiration to me and the team.

Carl, Rachel and I arrived early on Wednesday so we could visit the park before the Revival started. Toby became our guide and included part of the Indian reservation in our tour. While we were on "The road to the sun" in the mist of the majestic snow tipped mountain peaks, Toby said, "This is my fourth trip through here. Every time I come, I am overcome by God's great creation of another wonder of His world. I don't see how anyone could see this place and not believe in God's reality."

Toby and I went out together during our first visiting session on Thursday morning and had the privilege of seeing a young teen-ager pray to receive Christ.

God brought Toby and the others together for the Revival because He knew they would be needed to help grow and encourage the new church.

Like many Lay Led Revivals, the one at Hungry Horse had its own uniqueness. First, most of the fifty-five chartered members had been Christians for less the three months with no former church background. Drug problems, broken marriages, and a general unawareness of the love of our Lord had been the rule rather than the exception of many members before they experienced the new birth. Some families were surviving under third-world conditions—living in poor housing without running water or sanitary bathroom facilities.

The second thing that made this revival so unique was to see how God was using and blessing the faithfulness of Brother Andrew Goodwin.

For over two years he and his wife, Wanna, had labored without visible success. Along the way, he lost his voice when a very rare muscle spasm disease attacked his voice box. He wondered if God wanted him to keep on trying. But the Lord put him in touch with a specialist who prescribed a shot every three months which helped. "It takes a lot of energy to talk now because the sounds must come from deep within my chest. My speech is much slower and not as loud. But it has a good side. My ten minute sermons are now twenty minute sermons," said Brother Goodwin who hasn't lost his sense of humor. It didn't take a theology expert to recognize that the good things which were happening in Hungry Horse were because of the faithfulness of Brother Goodwin.

Not a day passed without someone being in Brother Goodwin's office (converted from the inner gambling quarters of the casino) seeking counseling about their problems and God's grace. For example, Hermann and I were paired with Rhonda during a visiting session. Rhonda wanted to visit a lady she had been thinking about.

God had prepared the lady and she was saved when we presented the plan of salvation. While traveling to our second house, I asked Rhonda about her salvation experience.

"I've only been saved about three months. My life has had its up and downs and I thought it might soon end when I learned I had a tumor the size of an egg in my stomach. I was plenty scared when I went to talk to Brother Andrew. He told me about Jesus and I prayed to be saved. When I went to have the operation, the cancer was gone. God healed me."

Rhonda's husband, Elmer, was present at the church every day, visiting or driving the van which had been donated by an Alabama church. Brother Goodwin told me about Elmer when we arrived. "He doesn't have running water at his house; but I hope one of your men can stay there. He hasn't been a Christian but three months, but already he has led two men to the Lord." Carl Howard was the man selected to stay in Elmer's home. His physical needs were taken care of at the church which has showers and bathroom facilities.

Brother Goodwin added, "At one home available to keep team members, the parents aren't Christians. Their son, Jesse, who is a member of the church wanted to keep someone and they agreed." Hermann and Bill, both making their first Lay revival, became their guests. God did a work in this home. The family, which had a multitude of problems, was attending church by the end of the week. Jesse, a loving all-around junior high athlete, was a natural leader with other children. He always had a ready smile and was a blessing to everyone around him.

Another young man whom God seemed to have

His hand upon was named Teal.

On Friday, when Hermann and Bill carried the youth on a picnic overlooking Hungry Horse Lake, Teal chose to stay and visit in the homes. Teal confided to me that he wanted to be a basketball player. I told him many basketball players became great in their backyard, practicing alone. "I have a ball but I don't have a goal," he replied. I knew the feeling about not having a ball or goal. I told him about walking many miles selling salve so I could get a basketball for my prize. I made a goal out of boards and a barrel hoop. However, when the basketball came I played with it only a few minutes before it bounced on top of a cotton stalk and burst. Teal's family didn't come to church. I surmised that money was short so I gave him enough to buy a goal and explained he could make his own backboard. Hopefully, the day will come when the church can afford recreational equipment for their youth, which seems to be their strength right now.

Rachel and I stayed in Lisa and Tiny Wegner's home located on the bank of the Flathead River. I wished for fishing tackle when Lisa told about catching an eight-pound rainbow trout in their backyard.

Tiny, a millwright, was working a shutdown in Idaho so we didn't get to know him.

Telling people about Jesus is serious business during a Lay Revival, but there are always the light moments. One happened during the final service on Sunday morning. The Lord brought Kathy from Kalispel to Hungry Horse to be the church's director of music. Kathy's husband was also working out of town and could not be at the revival to help with their three small children. Kathy, a very beautiful lady and a former "Mrs. Montana" was nursing her four-month-old baby when it was time to lead a song. I saw what was happening and changed the order of service until she was more available. It was refreshing to be in a new church where the program was not so rigid.

I believe God did want me and all the others to go to Montana. Each of us experienced God in our own way. If we have a chance to go again at some future day, we might see more concrete evidence of what God has been doing in Hungry Horse. What I'll always remember most about Hungry Horse is the faithfulness of Brother Andrew Goodwin and Wanna. Because of them, we had a chance to see what real missionary work is all about. Their sincerity almost brought tears to Rachel and me after the final service on Sunday evening when Brother Goodwin announced that everyone was invited into the fellowship hall (the former bar) for a party. We were never more surprised when they rolled out two huge cakes decorated with "Happy Forty-fifth Anniversary to Ernest and Rachel." I'd casually mentioned the date during our introductions on Wednesday night. Their thoughtfulness will always be a pleasant anniversary memory.

God works in the lives of His people in many mysterious ways. The story of Candy and her husband, Ian (I may not have his name exactly right), was a sidelight of the Hungry Horse Revival. It started Friday afternoon after visitation when I decided to walk out to the fruit stand near the church to buy some peaches. As I was about to leave the stand a lady walked up and we struck a conversation about the abundant huckleberries growing wild on the nearby mountainsides. As our conversation continued, it seemed natural to tell her about the revival in progress and share the magic cards. After having fun with the numbers game, I asked her if she knew about eternal life.

"I know Jesus and He lives in my heart," was her emphatic answer.

"I was a Hippie in the sixties and got involved in the cults. I was once demon possessed. But a friend prayed for me, and later took me to church where I was saved."

We shared our testimonies for several minutes. Then I turned to see a red headed man, taller than me, staring down over my shoulder. "This lady is my wife! What's going on here?"

Needless to say, I was quick to tell him we were talking about the Lord. His expression softened as I explained about the revival and invited them to attend the service which would start at seven.

Candy responded that they were on their way back to their ranch near Austin, Texas; but they might come if they could find a place to stay.

When the service started they were in a pew.

Everyone made Candy and Ian feel welcomed and they just joined our group. They were with us all day Saturday and at the service that night. But Candy was alone at Sunday School. I asked about Ian. She wasn't sure where he was. I could tell Candy was upset. "Are you two having some kind of trouble?" She could keep a straight face no longer. The tears rolled out as she said, "Ian is not a Christian!"

"Is Ian coming to church?" I asked.

"He said he might."

"Let's pray that God will bring him and save him," I said as we stood between the pews and had our prayer without regard to the people who were being seated.

God heard our prayer and Ian was there at church time but made no move during the invitation.

I was outside the building when Candy and Ian came by and said they were on their way back to Texas. I didn't know what else to say. I think I said something about it being a great service, that Barry had shared many wonderful experiences about the Lord.

"Awesome!" was Ian's only word.

"Ian, Candy told me you aren't saved. Jesus saved me in the middle of the ocean. He'll save you right here in front of this building if you want Him."

Tears came in Ian's eyes as He said, "Yes, I want Him."

The three of us embraced and I led Ian in the sinner's prayer.

A few people outside our circle knew what was happening. But nobody knew it like Ian as he shook my hand again and again.

Ian and Candy won't be members of the Hungry Horse Church. But the church can know they had a part in Ian's salvation by simply loving him and

Candy as God prepared Ian for salvation in their front yard.

Raising money to keep the building continued to be a concern for Brother Andrew. The Florida Baptist Association had sent $25,000. The final $88,000 was due by the end of September. The bank agreed to finance $50,000 if they could raise the $38,000.

Rachel had written a letter to the Alabama Baptist News expressing the need. It generated some giving. Two days before the deadline to keep the building, they still needed $34,000. That Sunday, the Camden Baptist church voted to send the balance—$34,000.

The Lord had led Bill Albritton to Montana so he could see the need and make his presentation to the Camden congregation. It will be interesting to see how God raises the final $50,000. He will! What He has started, He will complete.

LAY TEAM IN HUNGRY HORSE MONTANA. Left to right: HERMANN BRANDT, BARRY BARRETT, CARL HOWARD, BILL ALBRITTON, LOIS McELROY, HENRY McELROY, RACHEL DYESS, ERNEST DYESS, REV. ANDREW GOODWIN AND TOBBY SMITHERMAN.

29

God's Graduation Commencement

--I was a stranger, and you took me not in: naked, and you clothed me not: sick, and in prison, and you visited me not. (Matthew 25:43)

If you are a Christian, and God has been convicting you to share your faith more, this chapter is for you.

Sharing our faith starts with a commitment. I don't believe God will use us until we make a surrender of our will to be used by Him. That is why I often include an invitation, following a talk at a church, to just "Be Available" to be used by the Lord—to be willing to share Christ with those He puts in front of us in our daily activities.

When Christians are willing to tell others what Jesus is doing in our lives, the whole world will be won to Him in a short time.

I made that commitment in April of 1975. My life has not been the same since. Like most Christians, I've had my ups and downs. I've seen God's victories and I have lamented over my failures. But the victories and miracles God has let me see all had their beginning when I stood before my church and told my Pastor, Tommie Davis, "I want to be more of what God wants me to be."

Rachel and I joined the Lay Team which God used to help me make that decision. The early trips were learning experiences. I saw one-on-one witnessing, and heard other lay men and women share about leading the lost to Christ. I knew God was using my testimony while I was with the team, but I longed to have the first-hand blessings of seeing the lost come to Christ. We were on a revival in Murfreesboro, Tennessee when God showed me that He would grant my plea.

A lot happened that night. Barry Barrett, an American Airlines pilot, made a commitment to serve the Lord at the evening service. I didn't know Barry, but he would become a close friend, lay leader, and dynamic soul winner.

I don't recall their names, but Rachel and I were staying with a young couple who lived in an old family home near a lake. That night God sent me a vision when I lay down in the rustic bedroom. I seemed to be in the mist of a graduation service. The vision was clear as day. The stage was very plain with almost no decorations. But those receiving their diplomas were dressed in gorgeous blue gowns, trimmed in unbelievable white. One by one, they stepped forward from a long line to receive their diploma. There were no walls surrounding the stage. Only an endless line of graduates, who seemed to get smaller and smaller, as they stretched farther than the eye could see.

I thought about the vision. I knew the graduation service was not about a school. It was a service for those graduating into the halls of heavenly eternity. A graduation that comes when a person accepts Jesus Christ as his or her personal Savior. But what was my role, if any, in the vision? Then it all seemed to come together. Many of the people He would have me share the good news with would not come from affluent society. That was the reason for the plain graduation stage. Twenty-two years since that night in Tennessee, I have been seeing the fulfillment of that vision. The last two weeks have been very special.

Many times on Monday of the first week, I thought about the weekly prison ministry. I spent a lot of time in prayer. I went to my place under the pine tree and asked God to be ahead of me. I asked Him to make the prison ministry more than a Monday night ritual for Peyton Burford, Jimmy Simpkins, Jim Moree, and myself.

That afternoon I got involved in some farm activity and it was late when I got to the county jail. Jimmy was unable to come that night so I had the jail alone. I started in the big bull ring, the main compartment which houses about fifteen men.

People in this compartment come and go. They are not yet hardened criminals, but could easily get that way unless something happens to turn them around. They are the most reachable of all the inmates.

There are always some who are doing more time than others, who carry over from week to week. These men usually lead the way, putting up the card games, turning off the television, and getting their New Testaments which have been provided through the Gideons.

One of the men volunteered to lead in singing a couple of songs. I am sure we wouldn't have won any choir awards, but the singing stopped all the side talks and began preparation for what the Lord wanted to do that night. We concluded with "Amazing Grace". There's something about that song that not only lifts the believer, but also touches the heart of the lost. As we concluded, I could see the serious thoughts on the faces of everyone.

I don't even remember how the service began but I could feel the presence and power of the Holy Spirit as I spoke. We talked about the joy of heaven and what a wonderful place it is going to be. We referred to the words of the song and 10,000 years as only a beginning.

"If we only knew how wonderful heaven is going to be we would want to go there right now. The Bible says in I Corinthians 2:9 *The eye has not seen, nor the ear heard, nor the heart felt the wonderful things the Lord has prepared for those that love Him.*' But we can't go until God is ready for us. That's why He only gives us a glimpse of heaven.

"You see, He has a purpose for you and me. You may think tonight that your life has no purpose. That nobody loves you. That you are on a dead end street and that's why you got in jail. You have reached a point where you don't care what happens. But there is someone who cares and that someone is Jesus.

"I want you to look at everyone in this room. Do you see anyone who looks exactly like you? Is there anyone in the whole world who looks exactly like you? There is nobody! God made you unique. And if He made you unique, isn't it conceivable He made you for a purpose?

"I have been watching Billy Graham give press interviews about his life. One day he will finish his purpose for which God created him. Although there will never be another Billy Graham, there may be someone in this cellblock God wants to use in a way like Billy Graham. For most of us, God's purpose won't be like Billy Graham's.

"He may want us to be the janitor at a church, or a Sunday school teacher, or a papa to some wayward kid who doesn't even know his real daddy. I believe we will get the same reward in heaven that Billy gets, if we are faithful to God's calling."

God was powerful that night. I could see He was speaking to every man in the cellblock. They were thinking about their lives and the reality of heaven. It was time to tell them how to get there.

"God has used Billy Graham to reach more people than anyone before him, thanks to the medium of television. But God couldn't use him until he surrendered his life to be used. Billy had to come to Jesus Christ, just like you and me, before he could be used. Until we do that, we're not on His

229

side. We're still on Satan's side. Jesus said, '*I am the way, the truth and the life, and no man comes to the father except by me.*'

God provided that way through the cross. In spite of mankind's rebellion through Adam and Eve, God still loves His creation. Because He is just, He kicked them out of the garden, and we have been under a curse ever since. But God has provided a way back to Himself. That way is Jesus.

"John 3:16 reads, '*For God so loved the world, he gave his only begotten Son, that whosoever believes in him shall not perish, but have everlasting life.*' That verse is the key to heaven. When we accept Jesus and make Him our Lord, we won't perish, which means 'go to hell,' but shall have eternal life."

We spent the next several minutes talking about man's sinful nature and God's plan of salvation, then God led me share my own salvation experience. As I did, I asked them to open their Bibles to Psalm 107:23-30.

"My salvation came in a storm just like these verses talk about. When I was young, I was a merchant seaman. As verse 23 reads, the company I worked for did business in great waters. I got on a ship in Mobile, Alabama. It was loaded with coal destined for Italy. The ships in Bible days moved by sails that caught the wind. Our ship was powered by diesel engines. But we would see God's wonders in the deep, just as they did with sailing ships."

As I proceeded in telling my story, I let one of the inmates read the Scripture, a verse at the time. When he read about the stormy winds and waves in verse twenty-five, I described the waves as being higher than the trees when the hurricane hit our ship. The inmate read verse twenty-six describing the waves mounting up to heaven, then going down into the depths and their soul melting because of trouble. Then I related how it felt to ride a great wave and be able to see for miles, then drop like a rock to the depths below, as water covered the ship. The verse adds that their soul melted because of trouble. Verse twenty-seven said they reel to and fro, and stagger like a drunken man, and are at their wit's end. I demonstrated how a sailor had to roll with the ship to stand or walk. Then I knew it was time to make the comparison of the story to their lives.

"All of you in this building are in a storm. Storms come in many sizes and shapes. My storm was just like the one we're reading about. It happened exactly the way we're reading it. Although your storm is different, you're in one. Some of you are discouraged with life. You might even be thinking about ending it. Some of you see no hope of ever climbing out of the situation you are in. Life has no purpose. You are just wandering with the crowd. Some of you are here because you wandered with the wrong crowd. You are in a storm all right. One that can carry you to the depths of hell. But there is a way out. Let's see how in the next verse."

The inmate doing the reading had a strong voice. Very clearly he read, '*Then they cry unto the Lord in their trouble, and he bringeth them out of their distresses.*'

"Do you want out of your distresses and troubles

tonight? Are you ready to cry out to Jesus? That's what the sailors did in the Bible story. That's what I did in my storm. By the third day, the coal in the number three hold had caught fire from the rolling of the ship. The ship got so hot we could hardly stay on it. We put out the emergency signal and the boson said we might go under any time. I was where many of you are tonight. In a storm, about to go out into eternity without Jesus. Forever separated from the love of the Lord, on my way to the depths of hell. Oh, I believed in God. I had for a long time. I thought I would have plenty of time to get straight with the Lord later. Some of you are thinking that tonight. But when the boson made his round to tell everyone to be ready to abandon ship, I knew I might not have much more time.

"I didn't know much about the Bible. I knew Jesus died for my sins and that I was a sinner. I knew if I made Him my Lord and asked Him to forgive me of my sins, He would. That's what I prayed and He saved me. If you are willing to pray as I did, His word says he will save you too. The key is making Jesus Lord. Agreeing to follow His will and not your own. Being willing to let Him make you the new creature which the Bible promises. Do you want out of your storm? Let's read verses 29 and 30 to see what happens when we sincerely ask."

As the inmate read about God making the storm a calm and the waves still, I could feel Him speaking to every man. I returned to my own story.

"You know what happened when I asked Jesus to save me?" I asked and waited for the impact of the question to enter every mind.

"Just as we read, God calmed the waters. In a short while the waves didn't break over the ship anymore. The deck hands were able to control the fire. We continued our journey to Naples, Italy.

"I believe that storm was just for me.

"That's my story. But what about you? Are you ready to cry out to Jesus in your distress? Do you want Him to take you out of your storm?

"I am going to have prayer for you; then on behalf of the Lord, give you an invitation to come to Him."

Seven men held up their hands to receive Christ. I talked about every knee bowing and the seriousness of their commitment. Then they prayed for Christ to take them out of the storm.

I made four more cell visits that night. They seemed to be uneventful. But Isaiah said in Chapter 55, verse 11, that no witness is uneventful. It will accomplish His purpose. I saw that the following week.

Jimmy had already spoken to the big bull ring group when I arrived the next Monday night. There was a lot of noise when I went to the back part of the jail. Sometimes Satan makes an effort to destroy our witness, especially when he knows God plans to do a great work.

Satan was at work as I walked down the hallway to the back cells.

Loud voices came from the little bull ring as I tried to talk to the men in the first two cells. Three of the men had already asked for salvation. The fourth man said he wasn't saved.   I concentrated my talk toward him as the others listened. Then the loud voices turned to body blows. I could hear the licks being passed and the shouting got louder. The cell door banged as deputies entered the little bull ring from the front to restore order. Then a deputy and a trustee came to the back corridor where I was. They were looking for something. Then one of them said, "Here it is," as he picked up a small ice pick looking dagger from the floor.

After they left, I returned my attention to the young man who had indicated an interest in coming to Christ but had already said he didn't think he was ready.

"You're falling into Satan's hands because he's telling you to wait. That you will have plenty of time later. But you don't know that. You could be the one to get into a fight. None of us knows what tomorrow might bring. But if you have Jesus, you don't have to worry about tomorrow. Satan is here tonight because he doesn't want you to come to Jesus. Who are you going to listen to, Christ or Satan?

"I want to be saved," was his answer.

The voices were still loud in the larger cell next door as I again explained to the man what it meant to become a Christian. Then we fell on our knees and he prayed the sinner's prayer.

There were eight men in the larger cell. Most had been there for a while. When we had talked to them on previous nights, some had listened, some had not. After all the commotion and the fight, would they listen tonight?

One of the men was older, with early streaks of

gray in his hair. He was alone in the break area when I arrived. We had freely discussed the Scripture on previous visits. I felt like we related to each other. We didn't talk much about the fight. In our prison ministry, we don't usually try to get involved with prison life. Sometimes we have to let the prisoners know that our sole purpose for being there is to share the gospel. Everything we do has to go through the jailer. I asked him if the others were coming. He said they were. While we waited, I encouraged him to be the peacemaker since he was more mature.

All the men but one soon came to the break room. I silently prayed that God would give me the right words.

"It's been a hot day and night. When you have nothing to do, it's easy for tempers to flare. Satan likes for you to get that way. He likes to see people at each others' throats. Just as God is real, Satan is also real. He's been here tonight. The reason he has been here is because God wants to do something great. The book of Job tells about some of the things Satan likes to do.

"He likes to destroy lives. Job was a righteous man. God asked Satan what he thought about his man Job. Satan told God He had a hedge around Job. In other words, God was taking care of Job. 'If you take all his goods, he will curse you,' said Satan. To prove Satan wrong, God told him he could take all Job had. Later He included his health, but not his life.

"One after another Satan took all Job had—his livestock, children, and health. Even his wife told him to curse God and die. But Job knew something. He knew something most of you don't know tonight. He knew he had a Redeemer. He knew he would live again. Look at your hands. Look at your arms. That very flesh you are looking at will one day rot away and be no more. Even though Jesus had not yet been born, Job knew he had a Savior. God revealed it to him long before Christ came. '*I know my redeemer lives and shall stand at the latter day upon the earth: and though worms destroy this body, yet in my flesh shall I see God. (Job 19:25-26)*'

"The Holy Spirit comes to live within us when we accept Jesus. That's how we know we have eternal life. God wants you to invite Jesus into your life and get you out of the terrible storm you are in right now."

Again I felt the Lord wanted me to share my testimony along with Psalm 107:23-30. God led the same way He did in the big bull ring.

Five men came forward to receive Christ when the invitation was given.

God made their storm a calm. Now they can proceed to their heavenly destination.

I believe God was as powerful those two Monday nights as any time in my witnessing experience. There is no greater earthly reward than to know His presence and see His power. It doesn't matter if we are talking to heads of government or someone in jail, God loves each of His creation the same way.

30

"A Little Bird Told Me!"

And Jacob vowed a vow, saying, If God will be with me, and will keep me in this way that I go, and will give me bread to eat, and raiment to put on, So that I come again to my father's house in peace; then shall the Lord be my God. And this stone which I have set for a pillar, shall be God's house: and of all thou shalt give me I will surely give the tenth unto thee. (Genesis 28:20-22)

"My name is Annie Laurie Brown, Laurence McPherson's daughter. We want to invite you to be our guest speaker for homecoming service at Indian Springs Baptist Church May 3," said the pleasant voice on the phone.

Mrs. Brown went on to say that they had one service a year. "We meet to renew relationships and raise money to keep up the cemetery. We can

237

only give a small honorarium.

Annie Laura and I had never met, but the mention of her father's name brought a warm memory of a man I had featured in the *Perpetual Harvest* more than twenty-five years before. I quickly assured her that I felt honored to be invited and would donate the honorarium to the cemetery fund.

As May third drew near, I really didn't know what to expect at the homecoming. I happened to be in the barbershop and casually mentioned my invitation to Indian Springs to Vann Warren. Vann knew all about Indian Springs. He even had kin people buried there. Through the back roads, it was not far from where he was raised.

"It was once a thriving community, but most of the people have moved away," said Vann. "But 'Homecoming' is usually well attended," he added.

On Wednesday night, as I usually do when I have an upcoming speaking engagement, I asked my church to pray for me. After the service, Virginia (Hines) Cameron said Indian Springs was her former church. She planned to be there for homecoming. "I was baptized in the springs behind the church," she said.

May third was a beautiful spring day. A few miles after passing through McWilliams on highway 21, I saw the church sign with its 1834 organizational date. As I turned onto the gravel road for the three-mile drive to the church, I quickly realized the use of the land had changed from its former agricultural days.

Stands of tall majestic pine trees bordered each

side of the road. All that was left of a former culture was the occasional ruins of a fallen farm building visible through the undergrow h. I drove slowly, enjoying the beauty of the well managed forest. I could tell that the land was fertile and probably yielded a decent living to those who nurtured it in bygone days. But not a single residence remained.

I crossed a small valley, and there stood the church. Still a beacon of worship for those who would be there from far away places such as Texas, North Carolina, Florida and in between. I thought about the title of my message, "Back to Bethel." I felt it was the theme God wanted me to use.

Several cars were already on the grounds. I'd hardly parked before Mrs. Hines, Virginia's mother, came and introduced herself. She was one of those who hadn't left the Beatrice area. I soon met Mr. Massey, who had once lived in Suttle where I taught school. He and his wife now live in Magnolia Springs. I asked him to give me a tour of the cemetery. I wanted to know where Mr. Laurence McPherson was buried.

We'd hardly started when a lady with an arm full of flowers for the cemetery said, "I'm Annie Laura Brown. I have sickness in the family and regret I won't be able to stay for the service. James Hines from Selma will be the moderator and introduce you."

I asked Annie Laura about her father's grave and told her how much I had enjoyed knowing him. I could see she had inherited some of Laurence's warmth as we chatted.

James started the service promptly at 11:00 o'clock. The wooden pews in the one-room building were in good condition and reasonably comfortable. There were no electrical outlets and it didn't appear that electricity had ever come that way. Larger than most country churches, I guessed it would seat two hundred people. Following a brief business session and two songs, James said I could speak as long as I wanted, but the congregation planned to enjoy dinner on the grounds at twelve. I knew I had plenty of time.

I briefly shared some of my testimony related to going back to my "roots" when Uncle Bill died (chapter 27). I described the hardships rural families struggled with during the Great Depression. "I expect it was the same with many of you who lived here during that time. But like me, I can see by the way you are dressed, and the nice automobiles you drive, that God has blessed each of you just as He has me. Coming here today reminds me of one of the great phrases of the Bible when Jacob told his family, 'We must go back to Bethel.'

"Bethel is a place where we have had an experience with God. I expect this very building is bethel for many of you. If your experience was not in this church building, it might be somewhere in this community. If you know Jesus, you have been to Bethel. My Bethel was in the middle of the ocean," I said and briefly related my salvation experience at sea.

"Jacob had his Bethel experience when he was fleeing for his life from his brother Esau. First, Jacob had finagled his older twin brother out of his birthright. Then he and his mother, Rebekah, who loved Jacob, conspired to get their father Isaac's blessing. The father's blessing was sacred in those days and carried great power. Isaac was nearly blind and thought he was giving the blessing to Esau who was the rightful heir since he was firstborn.

"Esau cried when he realized Jacob had supplanted him two times, and made a vow to kill Jacob after his father's death. When Rebekah heard of the threat she sent Jacob to live with her brother in a far country. Jacob had his 'Bethel' experience after his first day's journey.

"Jacob dreamed that he saw a great ladder reaching from earth to heaven. Angels were going up and down the ladder. The Lord stood above it.

"Jacob awoke and was afraid. 'Surely the Lord is in this place and I knew it not.'" Titus 2:11 reads that the spirit that brings salvation appears to all. Just as God spoke to Jacob, I believe every person has a Divine Appointment with God. How we react during that appointment is up to us.

"Jacob named the place Bethel. He took a stone he had used for a pillow, poured oil upon it and vowed a vow. 'God, if you will be with me, and keep me in the way I go, and give me food to eat, and clothes to wear, and will bring me again to my father's house in peace, then you shall be my Lord and my God.'

"Jacob went to his uncle Laban's house, met his beautiful daughter Rachel, and fell madly in love. He made a deal with Laban to work seven years for Rachel. The Scripture says that the time seemed only a few days because of his love for Rachel. However, like Jacob, his uncle Laban was a schemer. When the wedding day arrived, he slipped his older daughter, Leah, into the honeymoon tent.

"When Jacob confronted Laban in the morning, Laban said, 'In our country, we cannot give the younger before the firstborn. Take Leah and work seven more years for Rachel.' The culture of those days allowed a man to have more than one wife.

"Time will not allow me to talk of all the things that happened to Jacob while he was in Laban's house. Let me just say that God blessed him in all that he did. Jacob worked for a share of the stock and accumulated sheep, goats, cattle, asses, and camels. When Laban became jealous and changed the rules, saying that he could only have the speckled offspring, they bare speckled. If he said the ringstraked shall be thy hire, then bare all the cattle ringstraked.

"After twenty years God spoke to Jacob and told him it was time to go home. He took his family and all his livestock and started the long journey, not knowing if his brother Esau still planned to kill him. When he got close to home, he received word that Esau was coming to meet him with four hundred men.

"Then Jacob was greatly afraid and distressed. He divided his family and livestock into two groups, thinking that if Esau destroyed one, the other might escape." The Bible says that he also did a lot of praying.

"When Esau came, he ran to Jacob, put his arms

around him, and they both wept. Esau had forgiven Jacob and welcomed his brother home.

"The parting of Esau and Jacob leads to the heart of the message I want to leave with you today. Not only were the brothers reconciled and Jacob was able to come in peace to his family again; but also he thought of the reason it had all happened.

"Jacob told his family in Genesis 35:3 *'Let us arise and go up to Bethel and I will make an altar unto God who answered me in my distress, and was with me in the way I went.'*

"God had done everything Jacob had asked. He had given him food. He had given him clothes. He had brought him again to his family in peace.

"The question we must each ask ourselves today is, 'Have I been back to my Bethel and thanked God for all He has done for me?' Just be sure you have a Bethel. If you have never come to Christ, you can come by simply asking Him to forgive your sins and make Him Lord of your life. You and God know where you stand.

"I want to close my remarks by telling you about a man I met several years ago. He is buried in this cemetery. He had found his Bethel.

"When I worked at MacMillan Bloedel, we did a feature article on Laurence McPherson. I was touched by his story of how he had started with a cow, sold her for a $20 gold piece, and over the years, parlayed that into 6,000 acres of land. Laurence was a civic-minded man. He took an old log house and made it into a museum, filling it with old artifacts. He later gave all this to the Monroe

County Heritage Museum. Mr. Laurence loved to travel. When I met him, he had just returned from a trip to Alaska with one of his sons. They made the trip in a pickup, sleeping under a camper shell. Mr. Laurence never got old. He was taking college courses in his seventies.

"When he was seventy-nine, he got sick and was admitted to the J. Paul Jones Hospital in Camden. A visitor related to me that he talked to Mr. Laurence during the weekend.

"'The doctor told me I could go home next week. But I am going home before then. A little bird told me,' said Laurence as he smiled and pointed upward.

"The next day Mr. McPherson died after a sudden heart attack. Somewhere in his life, he had been to his Bethel."

For me, God was still working after the service ended. I don't think I have ever been to a more bountiful church dinner on the grounds. A number of people spoke to me during the meal fellowship. One was a lady from Chipley, Florida.

I told the lady, "It just so happened that yesterday I met the Choir Director and Minister of Education from the Chipley Baptist Church at a family reunion in Loxley, Alabama. I have never met a man with more enthusiasm for his job than Brother Colletti, who is a distant cousin.

The lady excitingly replied, "I go to the same church! You're right, he is an enthusiastic person."

"I asked him to pray for our meeting today. You go back and tell him God heard his prayers," I said.

We both agreed that the Lord had been in our

midst as we worshipped. I also thought of how great God is to bring us together, many miles from Chipley, to a remote spot like Indian Springs because someone prayed.

Milton McPherson, Laurence's oldest son who is a member of the history department at Troy State University, came to me and said, "Daddy wrote his memories to his grandchildren before he died. Twenty years after his death, we decided it should be published and shared with others. If you would like to read it, I'll send you a copy. When you finish, write a brief review for the local paper, then give it to the Camden library."

The book, titled *Memories That Lingered*, proved what I had already guessed—Mr. Laurence was an unusual person.

Fiercely patriotic, Laurence served in both World War I and II. His service accounts are vividly described, especially his tour in the Navy Seabees and duty on Siapan. Included are many pictures and facts about the war.

Laurence worked his way through the University of Alabama. When he ran out of funds, he dropped out of school until he could earn enough to go back. Once he had enough money for tuition, but not for room and board. He solved that problem by setting up a tent on campus and living in it for a year and a half.

The book contains much rural Alabama history, especially from the viewpoint of a teacher who taught in one and two-room schools. He also coached for six years at my old high school, Robertsdale, during the early thirties. Later he was at Isabella and Maplesville.

In addition to Annie Laura and Milton, Laurence's other children are Bart, Larry, and Jimmie.

God's invitation to Indian Springs was a divine appointment for me in more ways than just the formal service.

INDIAN SPRINGS BAPTIST CHURCH, established in 1834, is typical of many once thriving rural churches in America.   The congregation still holds an annual homecoming in May.

31

What Shall I Do Lord?

And I said, What shall I do Lord? And the Lord said unto me. Arise, and go into Damascus; and there it shall be told thee of all things which are appointed for thee to do. And one Ananias—came unto me—and said, The God of our fathers hath chosen thee—For thou shall be his witness unto all men of what thou hast seen and heard. (Acts 22:10-15)

In my first book, *GOD, IF YOU'RE REAL, LET THE COW BE IN THE PEN WHEN I GET HOME*, and in this sequel, I have tried to tell you how God has been real in my life. I shared some of my innermost feelings with two objectives. First, if the reader has never accepted Jesus, I hoped my experiences might encourage the person to seek the Lord. Second, I wanted all Christians to catch a vision of sharing their faith with others.

God gave the commission to Paul to go and tell

the things he had seen and heard. I believe that same commission applies to all Christian lay men and women. Three times in the book of Acts we have a written account of Paul sharing his testimony. I believe he shared it every time he spoke. You may think you don't have a dramatic testimony to share like Paul. You didn't see a great light which blinded you with Christ's glory. But I submit that if you know Jesus, your testimony can be as powerful as Paul's. Let me share an example of this belief.

About every three months I get a call from a representative of the Alabama Agricultural Statistics Department. The organization makes on-going surveys about pecan, catfish, and other agricultural crops.

They hire about twenty-five ladies who do the calling as a part-time job. When they call about the status of my catfish and pecans, my standard reply is, "I'll answer your questions, if you will give me a couple of minutes when you finish." We usually reach an agreement.

"Now what did you want to ask me?" comes at her conclusion.

"If you were here with me, I might use some cards and play a little game with you and tell you how old you are. Then I would get serious and turn to the back of the cards and ask you a question, 'Do you know for sure you have eternal life?' How would you answer that question if you were with me?"

When I posed the question to one of my recent callers, she said, "Yes, I know I'm saved!"

"How long have you been saved?" was my next question as I sought to discover the foundation of her faith.

"Thirty-three years!" was her instant reply.

"Do you mind telling me how it happened?"

"It happened at church when I was seven years old. I felt I needed Jesus in my heart, so I walked down the aisle during the invitation and talked to my pastor. He prayed with me and I was saved."

"You have a powerful testimony," I said. "A majority of Christians can identify with you because they, like you, came to the Lord when they were young. That's the way it's supposed to be. Being born again and allowing Jesus to make us into a new creature is God's great miracle.

The Bible says He will draw each of us to him. People who didn't get saved until later years might have rejected Christ in their early years. You didn't do that. Accepting Jesus when He first calls is the way it should be. Your testimony is powerful! You said something tonight that made your commitment even more powerful."

"What was that?" she asked.

"You not only told me immediately that you were saved but you also said how many years it's been. Most people couldn't do that. If you had asked me, I would have had to do some figuring. Let me think—I was eighteen—now I'm . . . You said right away that you had been a Christian for thirty-three years. That was powerful! Every Christian has a powerful testimony."

Years ago, about 1973, I attended a "Win" school led by Dr. Earl Potts.

He said a testimony should contain three parts: (1) What we were before coming to Jesus; (2) How we came; (3) How our lives have been different with Jesus. During that school, we wrote a three-minute testimony using this outline. We were divided into small groups and shared our testimony, many of us for the first time. That exercise made a difference in my life. It could make a difference in your life if you too would write a three-minute story of what Jesus has done for you and begin to share it with those He puts in front of you.

If we think again about the conversion of Paul, we can easily recognize a critical point in his life. It was not when Ananias came to say that God wanted him to '*go and tell the things he had seen and heard.*' It was in verse ten when Paul recognized Jesus and said, '*Lord what would you have me do?*' That was when Paul made his commitment to serve the Lord. From that moment on, Paul was committed to follow Jesus.

Last weekend I led four witnessing conferences in Shocco Springs at a Pastor/Deacon/Spouse Retreat. In each session we talked about Paul's words after he recognized Jesus— '*Lord, what will you have me do?*'

Are you willing to ask Jesus "Lord, what would you have me to do with the rest of my life?" God might use you, like Paul, to change the world.

32

Moments of Doubt

When I consider thy heavens, the work of thy fingers,
the moon and the stars, which thy hast ordained; What
is man, that thou art mindful of him? And the son of man,
that thou visitest him? For thou hast made him a little
lower than the angels, and hast crowned him with glory
and honour. (Psalm 8:3-5)

It was almost dark when I walked into the pecan
house to weigh out some orders. It took a while
and the day had turned into full darkness when I
stepped outside into a moonless night. Before I
could move, I was drawn to an unusual brightness
in the clear sky. I thought I was seeing the lights of
flying airplanes as they sparkled through the
leafless pecan trees. Then I realized it was one of
those nights when a million stars seem to almost
touch the earth.

A rain, followed by a cool front, had passed

through the night before, clearing the atmosphere so I could behold the miracle of God's creation.

As I made my way to the house, I remembered our local newspaper had carried an article about how the planets of our own solar system had lined up in the Western Hemisphere. Tonight would be the perfect time to break out the new Nikon binoculars Rachel was giving me for Christmas for my deer hunting. As we sat down for the evening meal, I asked for them early so I could do some stargazing.

When I was a lad, before electric power lines were strung through the country blotting out the wonder of nightlife around us, my young friends and I would often lie on the grass on clear nights like this and watch for "shooting stars." We played all kinds of imaginary games as they shot their burning streaks billions of miles away. We never studied astronomy but we did know a few stars such as the Big and Little Dippers.

Stargazing is best away from all artificial light. Tonight, I felt the excitement of a kid with a new toy as I walked to the backside of the west pecan orchard, far away from the glare of our outside security light.

Looking through the binoculars, one star was so bright it hurt my eyes. It made me remember an evening at the camp house when I stepped outside and told Steve, "A car has gotten through the gate and is driving in." When the car didn't appear, I finally realized it was the evening star giving forth its brilliant light through the tops of the trees.

As my eyes became more accustomed to the

semi-darkness, I could see the Milky Way stretching from horizon to horizon. When I concentrated my lens on the flowing white mass, it became alive with hundreds of individual stars that my naked eye could not separate. I realized that every part of the Milky Way was in reality, a mass of planets which stretched endlessly in every direction of the universe.

I gazed for a long while. "What's really out there?" I thought. "Does the universe have an end? Is there a wall out there that God has placed to denote the end? I'd read somewhere that a scientist had numbered the galaxies. Did he have some formula that would indicate an end? Is heaven on one of the planets? How about life? We've sent people to the moon and robots to Mars. No life has been found there."

I wondered if Jesus felt the way I was beginning to feel when He spent forty days in the wilderness. When we reason with our minds, we think about beginnings and endings. If I had a rocket big enough, I could launch it toward the west, and it would be possible for it to circle the earth, and return to this very spot from the east. It would have a beginning and an end. But if I launched the same rocket toward outer space, it would never come back. If it was powerful enough, and could avoid the planets, would it go forever?

I didn't feel spiritually well as I walked back. Toward the house across the fish pond roadway. Satan had me in his mental wilderness.

Jesus quoted Satan Scripture when He was tempted. I remembered another time long ago when I'd agonized over reasoning about the universe and God's reality. An atheist professor had troubled my faith when I was attending Auburn University as he discussed, what he called, a godless universe.

One night God consoled me with Scripture as I walked along a dark part of the campus. He used the Scripture and brought to memory Jesus' conversation with Nicodemus after he asked about the way to eternal life. In the eighth verse of the third chapter of John, Christ used the illustration of the wind: *"The wind bloweth where it listeth, and thou hearest the sound, but canst tell whence it cometh, and whither it goeth, so is every one that is born of the Spirit."*

Like Nicodemus, I realized I didn't know all the answers. If I did, I would be like God. With that verse, God restored my faith when I was a young man. Years later He saved the professor which further confirmed His reality to me.

On this night, as my moments of doubt began to fade, I thought about Christ's promises. First, because of His death and resurrection by which I am redeemed, He has given me eternal life. He has further promised that He will never leave me or forsake me (Hebrews 23:5); That I am sealed until the day of redemption (Ephesians 4:30); And that nothing can pluck me out of His hand (John 10:28-29).

As I continued my walk back to the house, I realized just as I did long ago, that I will never fully understand about the stars and the universe until I am with Jesus. My moments of doubt passed.

Through the Scriptures, God returned the peace that passes all understanding.

Then God seemed to say, "Have I not verified my reality to you these many years? Have I not given you all these Divine Appointments you have written about in this book and the one before? Did I not arrange a Divine Appointment this very day?"

I'd spent much of the day pruning muscadines. I have to start in early December to finish by March. I was working on my first vine after lunch when the impression came that I should go to the house. I've long ago learned that when these thoughts come, I need to obey.

Rachel was in town that afternoon so I thought someone might be trying to get in touch. But the answering machine had no message. "Maybe someone is about to call. I'll rest my eyes and wait ten minutes." As I relaxed, I suddenly remembered that I was out of magic cards. If someone came I wouldn't have anything to give him. I looked through the house but couldn't find a set. Then I remembered we had a few packages of candy left over from our Christmas program at the jail. Each package contained a *Four Spiritual Laws* tract. I put a package in my truck and returned to the vineyard.

I'd hardly started working again when I saw a small truck coming down our gravel road. I went to the house and the driver identified himself as a sub-contractor helping Federal Express with their Christmas deliveries. "I brought you a package; please sign here."

We chatted a minute and I told him how to get to his next stop at Lower Peach Tree. "I know you

257

don't have much time but let me give you a Christmas present before you go," I said as I handed him the package of hard candy. "Usually I give visitors a little numbers game which include a question, 'Do you know for sure you have eternal life.' Do you have an answer for that question?" I asked.

"Yes, sir. I've been saved twice," he answered.

"How did you get saved twice?" I asked.

"I was baptized when I was a baby and confirmed when I was older," he replied.

"Tell him about Nicodemus," was God's clear thought to me. "The Bible says we must be born again to go to heaven. There is a story about a man named Nicodemus, a ruler of the Jews, who came to Jesus and asked how he could have eternal life. Jesus told him he must be born again. Nicodemus didn't understand how he could be born again. A lot of people don't understand about being born again. What Jesus was talking about was a spiritual birth," I quickly explained.

"We can't be saved until we realize we are lost. We have to come to a realization that we are sinners. We have to understand that we can't go to heaven like we are. That's why Jesus had to die on the cross. We can only be made clean through His shed blood by which we are redeemed," I emphasized.

I could see a troubled look on the man's face. It was easy to see that God was speaking to him.

"I've been out of church but I'm going to a different church now," he commented as we continued to talk about the plan of salvation.

"I know you need to go. I want to give you something that will further help you understand what we have been talking about," I said as I handed him the *Four Spiritual Laws*. Ours was indeed a Divine Appointment.

In this book and the original, I have written about Divine Appointments with the hope that you may more easily recognize the Divine appointments God has prepared for you.

God knows I have tried to be honest, without exaggerations. I believe God is big enough that we don't have to exaggerate anything He does. When possible and practical, I have used real names and places so anything I have written can be verified.

I've shared some of my weaknesses because I believe every Christian, in some way, is weak. I've written about my "Top of the Mountain" experiences as well as my time in the valley. For the most part, this chapter has been a deep valley. I delayed a while about writing it, thinking it is not a good way to finish a book. "Committed Christians shouldn't have doubts like I did when I thought about the endless universe," was my thought. But the proclaimer of Christ, John the Baptist, had doubts when he was in prison. Perhaps you have had your own doubts. Christ reassured John through His disciples. He reassured me. I believe He will reassure you if you ever have such a need.

I have written both books for the same purposes. First, to help the lost find Christ. If you have never come to Jesus, many of the chapters show you the way. If you still have questions, Dr.

Bill Bright's *Four Spiritual Laws*, which can be purchased at most Christian bookstores, will make the way plain. If you still question God's reality, ask Him to reveal Himself to you. He promises that you will find Him if you seek Him.

Secondly, I hope every Christian has caught a vision of sharing the love of Christ with a lost and dying world. If you are willing to tell the Lord that you are "available" for Him to lead you to share, I believe He will provide the tools and the way. Always remember that the greatest miracle you know about is your own salvation experience.

I don't know many details of her life, but Carla Faye Tucker is one of the greatest examples of God's power to make us all into new creatures. Most people haven't murdered someone like she did. However, the Bible says that we have all sinned, and without redemption through the blood of Jesus Christ, we cannot go to heaven. So our fleshly condition, without Christ, is also lost. But someone told Carla Faye about Jesus during her fifteen long years of waiting for execution. She accepted what Jesus did for her on the cross and the "new creature" began to emerge in her life, just as happens to every Christian.

The national news media picked up her story. Larry King, and a host of others, probed about her newfound faith. Some well-known evangelists sought to stay the execution because she had found Christ.

I only saw her on television once, about a week before the execution date in a Texas prison. The reporter asked if she thought her life should be spared.

"The Bible speaks about the mercy Christ showed to many people. Yes, I hope the courts will show mercy to me," she said with a sweet smile on her face.

But the courts did not change the conviction and Carla Faye died of a lethal injection in February of 1998. A reporter wrote about her last words to relatives and friends a few minutes before her death.

"I'm about to go and be with Jesus. I'll be looking for all of you to join me some day."

That's a powerful testimony of the reality of Christ and life after this life. God wants every Christian to have the same faith and assurance as Carla Faye.

God gave Carla Faye the opportunity to tell her last testimony six minutes before her death. He gives us the rest of our life to share our story to a lost and dying world.